SPiRiT

CrAfTS

5005 Spirit Crafts
This edition published 1997 by CLB International
Distributed in the U.S.A. by BHB International, Inc.
30, Edison Drive, Wayne, New Jersey 07470

© 1997 CLB International
A Division of Quadrillion Publishing Limited

Created by **ANTHOLOGY**, Brighton,
Sussex, England.

For Anthology:
Concept, Editorial, and Design Direction:
Rhoda Nottridge
Project Management: Jo Richardson
Design and Artwork: Wayne Blades
Photography: Steve Tanner
Illustrations: Michael Hill
Contributing Author/Craftmaker: Jan Eaton
American Adaptation: Josephine Bacon
Indexer: Ingrid Lock

For Quadrillion:
Editorial: Siobhán Creswell
Production: Neil Randles, Karen Staff,
Ruth Arthur

ISBN: 1-85833-660-0
Printed and bound in Singapore

SPiRiT CrAfTS

CHERYL OWEN

CLB

CoNtEnTs

InTRoDuCtioN

In this rapidly changing world, in which we are fast losing touch with our own history, it is fascinating to discover the spiritual origins of the crafts we take for granted and those that are unfamiliar to our culture. Many designs denote spiritual symbols, and it is awe-inspiring to find that many of the same basic symbols occurred thousands of miles apart, used by races that had never met.

All peoples have their particular gods and myths, but as different tribes and sects intermingle, so their religions and legends blend and enrich one another's cultures. In this way, many sacred symbols and stories have taken on similar interpretations in different religions. Certain Christian beliefs have evolved from paganism, while the ancient Greeks and Romans shared the same gods, although generally known by different names. Hinduism and Buddhism also overlap in some practices and convictions.

This book presents a wide range of crafts from all over the world that have powerful spiritual and symbolic significance. Their fascinating origins and meanings are fully explored, and concise step-by-step instructions and photographs help you to recreate ancient heirlooms and accomplish contemporary interpretations of traditional designs. Interspersed throughout the book are collections of beautiful, mystical symbols on a variety of traditionally popular themes, to inspire you to design your own personalized spirit crafts.

Tools and Equipment

Most of the projects in this book use only basic, everyday equipment, so you may already possess most of it. Always work on a clean, flat surface that is well lit, and keep any sharp implements, glues, and paint beyond a child's reach.

Drawing tools

Use an HB pencil for drawing. Keep pencils sharpened to a point for accuracy, or use a propelling pencil. Use a ruler and triangle when drawing squares and rectangles so that the lines are straight and the angles accurate. Use a pair of compasses to draw circles. A fade-away fabric marker is recommended for drawing on fabric – the ink will soon fade.

Cutting tools

Sharp, pointed scissors are indispensable for craftwork. Choose a pair that feel comfortable to work with. Use dressmaking scissors for cutting fabric but not to cut paper, since it will blunt the blades. Pinking shears will prevent fabric from fraying. They also give an attractive zigzag edge to the cut.

Craft knives and scalpels give a clean cut on paper and card. Always use a craft knife on a cutting-mat. Cut straight edges against a steel ruler. Do not attempt to cut tissue paper with a craft knife – it will probably tear. Plastic cutting-mats are available from art stores and major stationery stores. The surface is self-healing, so it can be used repeatedly. It is also slower to blunt the blades than other surfaces. Alternatively, improvise by cutting on a piece of thick card. Change blades regularly, since a blunt blade will tear the surface.

Use wire-cutters to cut wire, although an old pair of scissors will suffice. Use an old pair of scissors to cut fine metals. Any sharp edges can be smoothed off with a metal file. Use a hacksaw to cut cleanly through wood.

Adhesives

Always follow the adhesive manufacturer's instructions closely and test it first on any scraps. Use a plastic spreader to distribute glue evenly, or use a strip of card. A glue-gun is worth investing in if you plan to do a lot of craftwork. It is quick and easy to use and will stick many materials.

All-purpose household glue will stick paper, card, fabric, feathers, and most lightweight craft accessories, such as beads and natural dried materials. Latex glue will stick fabric and threads. Paper glues in stick form are clean and easy to use, but will only work effectively on paper materials. Masking tape is useful for temporarily sticking work in position. Use a low-tack masking tape and check that it will not tear or mark the work.

Spray-glue gives an even coverage of adhesive. It is suitable for paper, card, and fabric. Protect the surrounding area with newspaper and work in a well-ventilated room. Always use sprays that are free of CFCs.

PVA (polyvinyl acetate) medium is available from art and craft stores. It is a non-toxic adhesive that dries to a clear, glossy finish. Thin PVA medium with a little water to use when making papier mâché.

Superglue (strong epoxy resin) is very strong and will stick paper, card, metal, wood, fabric, and some plastics. Use superglue sparingly and handle very carefully. A gel superglue is easier to control than the liquid variety. Store superglue upright to prevent clogging.

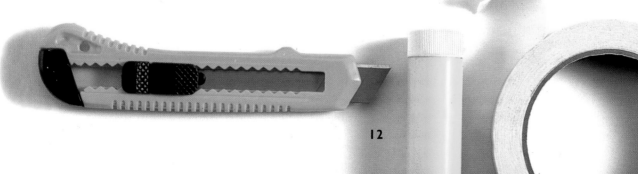

Painting tools

A range of paintbrushes will be needed if you plan to do a lot of craftwork. Good quality artist's brushes are worth the expense. Use a fine artist's brush for detailed work. Always clean brushes well immediately after use. Use a stenciling brush for stenciling. Paints can be mixed on an old china plate or a ceramic tile. Silk paint outliner is applied from a bottle with a fine nozzle or nib. Clean the bottle with cold water after use. Silk paints can be applied with cotton buds or paintbrushes.

A badger-hair varnishing brush is best for varnishing, but a good quality paintbrush would also be suitable.

A plastic carrier bag cut open and laid flat makes a good water-resistant surface to paint on.

Modeling equipment

Store clay that is not in use in an airtight container. Model the clay on a wooden cutting-board. The clay can be rolled out flat with a rolling pin and cut and modeled with a small knife.

Needles

For best results, use a needle suitable for the thread and fabric you are using. Straw (milliner's) needles are long and thin and therefore ideal for picking up a number of beads at a time. Needlepoint needles are thick and blunt, and suited to open-weave fabrics and mesh interlock canvas. Use a thick needle to make holes in clay and card.

Frames

To keep fabric taut, stretch it over a frame. Frames are available in various styles and sizes – some are adjustable in size. Stretch silk to be painted on a silk or batik frame, and protect the top surface with masking tape. The silk is held with 3-point silk pins, which will not damage the weave. Embroidery frames or hoops will prevent the fabric or interlock canvas distorting while you are working.

Materials

The projects in this book use a wide variety of exciting materials. Some you may already have, while specialist materials are available from art and craft stores. Other materials can be responsibly gathered from nature.

Natural materials

The garden or yard can supply a charming array of materials. Fresh foliage, dead wood, herbs, and discarded feathers will inspire rustic creations. Even string can be used creatively. Use eggs to make keepsakes, or collect shells left by the tide.

Paints and varnishes

Craft paints are very versatile. They are usually acrylic-based, the colors mix easily, give good coverage, and dry quickly. Most are non-toxic. Artist's acrylic paints are water-soluble when wet but water-resistant when dry. The paint dries quickly to a matte finish. Designer's gouache is a water-soluble tube paint that is thicker and more opaque than acrylic and watercolor paint. Latex paint is an opaque household paint available in a wide range of colors. It can also be applied as an undercoat when using other types of paint.

Most fabric and silk paints are washable and dry-cleanable after they have been heat-set with an iron. The outliner or gutta used in silk painting works as a resist to the paint. Use ceramic paints on china and glass, and clean the paintbrushes with mineral spirits before changing to another color.

Many of the projects are varnished for protection. Choose a varnish to suit the material or paint finish. Polyurethane varnish, available in gloss, satin, and matte finishes, is hard-wearing, although it does have a yellowing effect. Water-based varnishes are quick-drying and dry to a clear finish. Always varnish in a dust-free environment.

Wax, clay, and metals

Beeswax is used in candlemaking and to strengthen thread. Batik wax is available in granular form; the wax is melted and applied as a resist to fabric.

Air-drying clay is available from art and craft stores in natural white or terra-cotta. The clay can be painted with craft paints (ssee page 52), although the warm terra-cotta color is very attractive when left unpainted.

Thin-gauge copper and other metal sheets can be embossed or painted. The Hand of Fatima Amulet on page 38 is made from a metal tomato paste tube.

Needlework materials

Aida is a fabric of evenly-woven blocks with holes in between. It is ideal for cross-stitch embroidery because each cross stitch will fit over a block. Mesh interlock canvas is an even-weave canvas used for needlepoint. Work a complete tent stitch over each intersection of the mesh.

Stranded cotton embroidery thread is available in skeins in a wide variety of inspiring colorways. A skein is made of six strands which can be applied as one or as separate strands. Tapestry yarn is made of wool, and is available in skeins, again in a range of colors.

The small glass or plastic beads called rocailles are inexpensive and available in small quantities from craft stores and haberdashery departments. Available in a variety of vibrant colors, rocaille beads are very versatile – they can be sewn, threaded to make jewelry, or even glued in patterns onto bowls (see pages 72-73) or boxes.

Paper and card

The paper projects in this book use paper and card that is inexpensive and readily available. The thin card that cereal packets are made from is ideal for making templates that can be used repeatedly.

Colorful tissue papers can be made into delicate three-dimensional creations. Tear newspaper into strips to create papier mâché, which is surprisingly hard-wearing (see pages 96-97). Stencil board is a waxed card for making stencils. Ordinary thin card can be used as an alternative but is not as long-lasting.

Techniques

These pages present the basic techniques that occur in many of the projects. Read the instructions carefully and practice the various skills on a trial piece of work before embarking on any of the projects, for added confidence.

Using a template

Useful templates for many of the projects appear on pages 102-105. Trace the template onto tracing paper and mark the details. To transfer the design to another surface, either cut it out and draw around it or redraw the image onto the other side with a pencil. Tape the tracing face down with low-tack masking tape. Redraw to transfer the image. Cut the template from thin card to make a lasting template.

Using a craft knife

Work on a cutting-mat set on a flat, stable surface. Do not press too hard or attempt to cut right through the card at the first approach, but gradually cut deeper and deeper. To score card when making greeting cards, do not cut right through the card but break the top surface only, so that the card folds smoothly along the scored line. Cut straight edges against a steel ruler.

Modeling with clay

Knead the clay to make it pliable before you start modeling it. Many components begin as balls of clay. These can be rolled between the palms of your hands, then rolled into ovals, or molded into other shapes. Use a rolling pin to roll the clay evenly out flat on a wooden cutting-board.

Making a tassel

❶ Tassels add a decorative finishing touch to some of the projects. Cut the threads twice your chosen finished length of tassel, plus 1¼ inches. Fold another length of thread in half and insert its ends through a needle. Fold the tassel threads in half and pass the needle through the folds. Pull the needle through the loop to suspend the tassel.

❷ Thread the needle with a single length of thread. Bind the thread tightly around the tassel below the top. Insert the needle down between the binding thread and the tassel to secure it. Cut off the excess binding thread, then trim the lower edge of the tassel level. If using stranded cotton embroidery thread, separate the strands with a needle.

Cutting a bias strip

The bias is the diagonal 45° angle to any straight edge of fabric. Strips of fabric cut along the bias are used to bind seams and to make fabric cords that can be used as handles and button loops.

❶ Lay the fabric out flat and make sure the edges are straight. Fold one edge to meet the edge adjacent to it. Mark with a pin at each end.

❷ Open the fabric out flat again and use a ruler to draw a line between the pins. Mark the fabric into strips parallel with the diagonal line. Cut along the lines.

Cross stitch

Work each row of cross stitch over two journeys. Work a row of diagonal stitches from left to right, then complete the crosses with a second row of diagonal stitches worked in the opposite direction. Make sure that the top diagonal stitches all face in the same direction. Work from the center of the fabric ouward, and embroider one stitch on the fabric for every colored square shown on the chart (see page 106). Each stitch should be worked over one woven block of fabric.

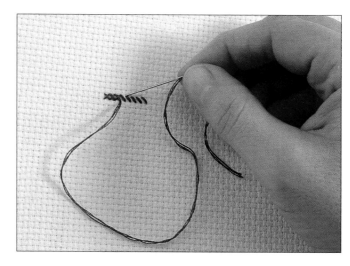

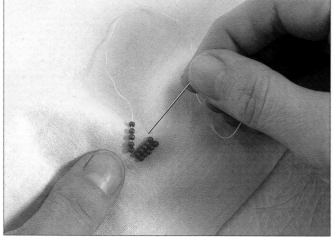

Lazy squaw stitch

This is a quick way of attaching beads to fabric. It can be worked in neat rows, as shown, or in a more random manner across the fabric. Bring the thread through the fabric and thread several beads onto it. Take a long stitch from right to left, then work a short vertical stitch to anchor the beads. Repeat, working from side to side.

Tent stitch

This is a small needlepoint stitch worked over one canvas intersection. Begin at the top of the shape and work a row of diagonal stitches from right to left . Work the next row beneath the first, working from left to right. Work from the center of the fabric outward, and embroider one stitch for every colored square shown on the chart (see page 106).

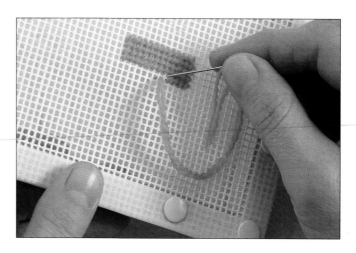

CHAPTER ONE
NaTurE's BoUntY

Native American Dream-Catcher
Spiral and Circle Symbols
Sacred Spiral Candles • Magical Shell Mirror
Engraved Gift Eggs • Aboriginal Dreamtime T–Shirt
Amazonian Feather Lampshade

The natural world offers endless scope, in terms of both materials and inspiration, for creating timeless ornaments and meaningful gifts. Embodying nature's very essence of serene beauty, feathers, stones, and shells that combine tactile texture with subtle color will harmonize with any decor, and impart comfort and reassurance. The elemental symmetry of eggs, complemented by colorful folk art designs, can bring a sense of new life and vitality to your home, while the warm, glowing light and sweet fragrance of beeswax candles create atmosphere and mystique. A simple T-shirt can be enhanced with a rich, bold motif adapted from an Aboriginal tree-bark painting, which resonates with the power of this ancient people's Ancestral Beings, the creators of all living things.

Native American Dream-Catcher

You will need

thick wire

masking tape

1 ³/₄ yards brown bias
binding

all-purpose household glue

dressmaking pins

thick cream thread

2 ¹/₃ yards brown suede
thonging

1 ³/₄ yards blue suede
thonging

27 large-holed wooden
beads

selection of feathers

To Native Americans, the circle symbolizes the cyclical nature of traditional cosmology. They believe that the earth is a circle, below which there is the circle of the sky, and inside these circles there are powerful spiritual centers. For this reason, the dream-catcher is circular, with a powerful center.

A dream-catcher, hung over a bed or on the door, prevents evil from entering the soul of a sleeping person. As the nasty thoughts try to push into the mind, the powerful circle catches them like a net, and protects the sleeper from having bad dreams.

Decorating a dream-catcher with favorite feathers, stones, shells, and anything gathered from nature makes it more able to personally protect its owner, or the person for whom the dream-catcher is destined.

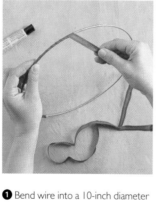

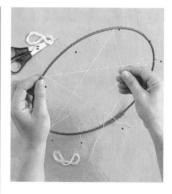

❹ Knot two lengths of blue thonging to the sides of the ring. Slip beads onto the thonging. Single beads can be secured along the lengths with a dab of glue. Fix beads and feathers to the ends.

❶ Bend wire into a 10-inch diameter circle. Overlap the ends and bind together with masking tape. Bind the ring with bias binding, gluing the ends in place.

❷ Divide the ring into tenths and mark with pins. To make the web, tie thread to the ring at the top division. Loop the thread tightly around the ring at the fourth division. Continue around the ring, looping the thread around the ring at every fourth division, to form a star. Tie to the ring at the starting point. Work another star in the same way at the remaining divisions, and thread on a single bead before completing.

❺ Tie or glue shells to the ring at each side. Suspend the dream-catcher on brown thonging, and knot the ends for hanging. Knot a length of brown thonging at the top, and slip beads onto the thonging, gluing in place as before. Knot the ends.

❸ Fasten three lengths of brown thonging to the bottom of the ring with a lark's head knot, as shown in the photograph. Thread three beads onto one end of one of the lengths, then hold the shaft end of a feather against it. Slide the beads over the feather to secure. If the feather shaft is very slender, glue it to the thonging first. Fix a short feather to the other end with a single bead. Complete the remaining thonging lengths in the same way.

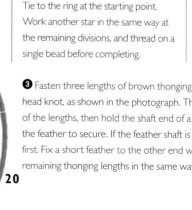

Spiral and Circle Symbols

The continuous, flowing line of the spiral and circle lends itself to many craft applications, especially those using natural materials. Foliage and flowers can be arranged as round garlands, either formally or at random, in a wild, free style.

Circle in a Square
The circle enclosed by a square symbolized a person's entire being in the magic of the ancient Orient. The circle represented the indestructible human spirit, and the surrounding square, the mortal body.

Stone Circle
The meaning of these manmade erections is uncertain. They are probably religious sites, the circle representing the cosmic eye of the Great Goddess. The medicine wheels of North America are often arranged like spokes of a wheel, and are thought to commemorate the dead. Some evidence gives astrological meanings to other stone circles.

Tai-Chi
This circular symbol of Eastern origin encompasses the opposing but balancing forces of "yin" and "yang." Each force contains an element of its opposite – for example, good and evil. It is often shown within magic symbols.

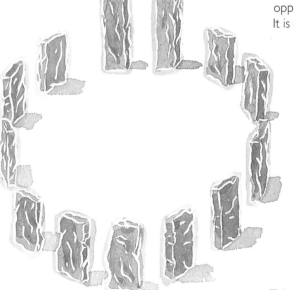

Spiral
Many ancient cultures believed that forceful energies flowed in a spiral, and a spiraled snake stands for creative energy. It is a powerful, dynamic motif offering wide decorative scope for a range of craft applications.

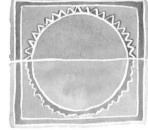

Divided Circle
This symbolizes the contrary qualities of hidden potential in the lower half and aspiration of a higher state above. Use it to present two complementary or contrasting designs.

Sacred Spiral Candles

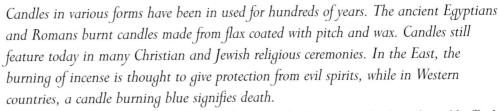

You will need

sheet of beeswax
hair dryer (optional)
craft knife
steel ruler
cutting-mat
candle wick

Candles in various forms have been in used for hundreds of years. The ancient Egyptians and Romans burnt candles made from flax coated with pitch and wax. Candles still feature today in many Christian and Jewish religious ceremonies. In the East, the burning of incense is thought to give protection from evil spirits, while in Western countries, a candle burning blue signifies death.

Beeswax has long been held in high esteem. In the past, only the rich could afford to burn candles of beeswax — the poor burnt tallow. The Mother Bee has links with Demeter, the Greek goddess of fertility. Consequently, honey is regarded as an aphrodisiac and denotes fertility. These beeswax candles are surprisingly easy to make.

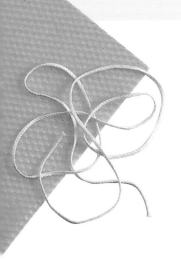

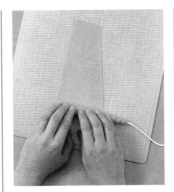

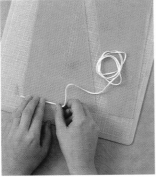

❸ Cut off a short sliver of beeswax along the lower straight edge, and set it aside to prime the wick later. Lay the wick along the longest side edge with the excess extending at the top.

❹ Carefully roll the sheet around the wick. When you have finished rolling up the entire sheet, gently press the short edge against the candle to stop it unraveling.

❶ Beeswax sheets are usually pliable enough to handle at room temperature. If the sheet is not soft enough to be pressed easily between your fingers, it can be gently warmed with a hair dryer for a few minutes.

❷ To make two spiral candles, using a craft knife and steel ruler, and working on a cutting-mat, cut diagonally across the beeswax sheet 2 inches from two opposite corners.

❺ Trim the wick to ¹/₂ inch in length, and rub with the sliver of beeswax to prime it ready for lighting. Two sheets of differently colored beeswax can be layered together to make the two-colored spiral candles. To make a straight candle, simply use a rectangle of beeswax rather than cutting the sheet diagonally.

You will need

framed mirror
selection of shells
glue-gun or superglue

Magical Shell Mirror

Shells represent the female, and denote birth and resurrection. Venus, the Roman goddess of love, was born from the foaming sea and swept ashore on a scallop shell. Scallop shells appear on Victorian valentine cards because of their association with the goddess of love. The scallop shell also has connections with the Christian religion.

In the East, the conch shell is thought to have magical qualities. It is worn by married women in the Gangetic states of India, and is sacred to Vishnu in Hinduism. In Buddhism, it represents the sound of Buddha.

Decorate a plain mirror with beach-combed shells, or use shells from a reputable specialist shell shop that does not sell shells of endangered or protected species.

❶ Arrange the shells on the mirror frame, beginning with the largest shells.

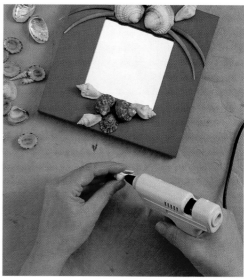

❷ Use a glue-gun or superglue to stick the shells in place on the frame.

❸ Glue tiny shells onto any remaining open areas of the frame.

Engraved Gift Eggs

You will need

eggs
large, sharp needle
bowls
fabric dyes
pencil
damp cloth
craft knife
fine ribbon
large-holed beads

Eggs symbolize creation all over the world, and have been presented as gifts for centuries. According to pagans, the sun dies in winter and is reborn in spring, when children distribute hard-boiled eggs as a declaration of new life. In ancient China, painted eggs would be handed out by generous rulers, and today, decorated eggs feature widely in religious festivals. Painted eggs are filled with confetti in Mexico to celebrate New Year. Traditionally a peasant pastime, the art of engraving eggs is practiced in many European countries, where they are hung from branches. These stylized eggs have been colored with fabric dyes and gently engraved with a craft knife.

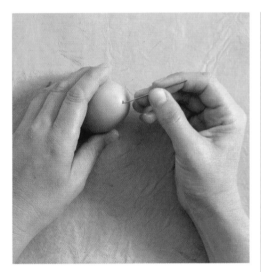

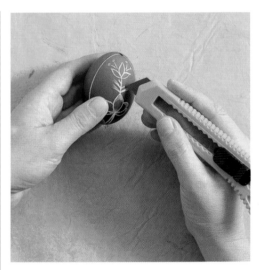

❶ Gently scratch both ends of an egg with a needle to make a small hole. Make one hole ¹/₄ inch wide and the other ³/₈ inch wide. Poke the needle through the larger hole into the egg to break the yoke.

❷ Hold the egg over a bowl and blow through the small hole to empty the contents of the egg into the bowl. Cover, and refrigerate the contents for use in cooking.

❸ Prepare a small dye bath following the fabric dye manufacturer's instructions. Color the egg with a strong solution of dye. Rinse and leave to dry.

❹ Draw a simple design on the egg with a pencil. Any pencil mistakes can be wiped off with a damp cloth. Alternatively, engrave a design directly onto the egg. Using a craft knife, gently scratch the design onto the egg, employing short strokes of the knife tip to build up the design.

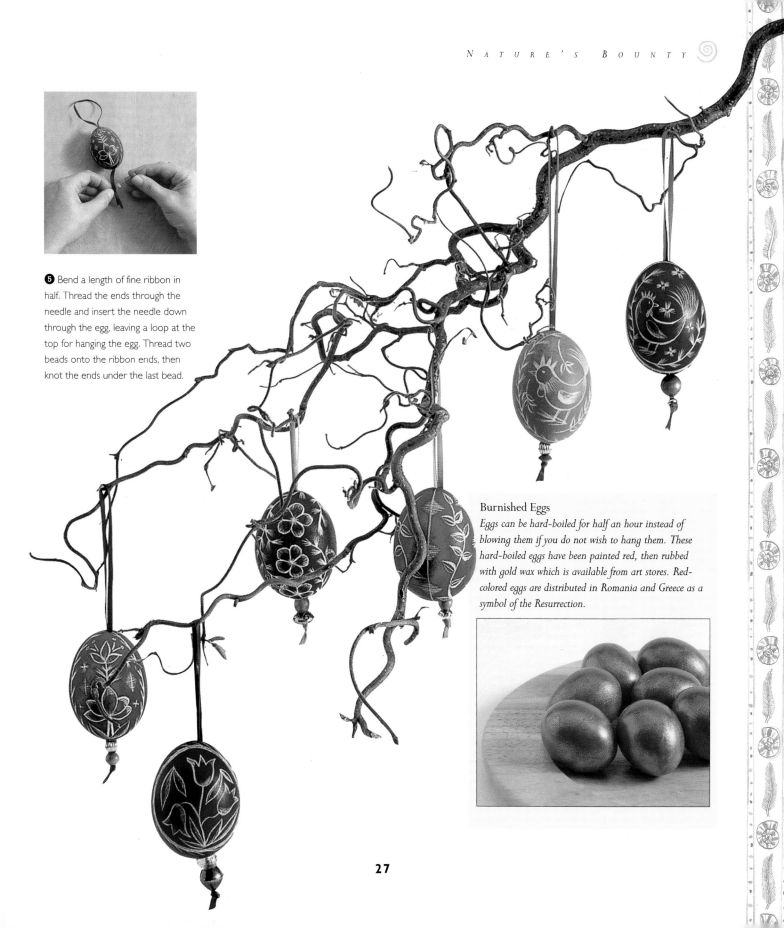

❺ Bend a length of fine ribbon in half. Thread the ends through the needle and insert the needle down through the egg, leaving a loop at the top for hanging the egg. Thread two beads onto the ribbon ends, then knot the ends under the last bead.

Burnished Eggs

Eggs can be hard-boiled for half an hour instead of blowing them if you do not wish to hang them. These hard-boiled eggs have been painted red, then rubbed with gold wax which is available from art stores. Red-colored eggs are distributed in Romania and Greece as a symbol of the Resurrection.

Aboriginal Dreamtime T-Shirt

Traditional Aboriginal art from Australia flows from the concept of the "Dreamtime" or "Dreaming," which is the cornerstone of their native culture. The Dreamtime is the time before history began, when the Aborigines' Ancestral Beings walked the earth, forming the landscape and creating all the plants, living creatures, and peoples of the known world. Images of the Ancestral Beings and of their travels, lives, and experiences form the largest source of imagery in Aboriginal art. Dreamtime images were traditionally painted on rock slabs, sheets of eucalyptus bark, and on flat areas of ground made from crushed termite mounds.

Bark painting is thought to be one of the oldest types of Aboriginal decoration. The bark is removed from the tree, scraped clean, and the design painted with crushed red and yellow earth, charcoal, and other natural pigments mixed with water and a fixative (originally orchid juice, now usually synthetic wood glue). The stylized fish on this T-shirt is typically shown in profile, surrounded by bands of dotting and cross-hatching.

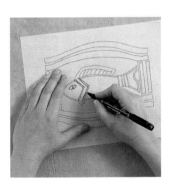

❶ Enlarge and trace the template on page 102 to the correct size. Using the thick marker pen, draw over the design so that all the lines are thick and black. Tape the design to the card and slip it inside the shirt. Adjust the card until the design is in the desired position, then transfer the motif to the shirt, using the pencil or the fade-away marker.

❷ Take the card out of the shirt, remove the design, then re-insert the card into the shirt, positioning it beneath the transferred design. Stir the fabric paints thoroughly. Using the photograph as a color guide, apply the first color with a small brush. Leave to dry, then apply the remaining colors in the same way, making sure you allow each color to dry before proceeding to the next. Finally, add dotting and cross-hatching details to the borders.

❸ Sign the shirt with your name or monogram in gold. Leave to dry overnight. Replace the card with a clean piece, positioning it underneath the painted motif. To fix the colors, cover the motif with a sheet of white tissue paper or parchment paper, and press with a hot iron.

Amazonian Feather Lampshade

You will need

plain lampshade
dyed feathers
all-purpose household glue

The brightly colored feathers of toucans and scarlet macaws are much prized by the tribes of the Amazon basin. The men wear flamboyant feathers, the colors and type of these feathers having special meanings. The birds of the Amazon are revered, and bird spirits are said to be messengers between the Earth World and the benevolent Sun. Feathered headdresses and wings of plumes are worn by the men in ceremonial dances to emulate birds visiting from the Sky World.

This vibrant feather lampshade is inspired by the magnificent headdresses made by the Amazonian Trumai tribe. Brightly colored dyed feathers are available from craft stores or suppliers. Alternatively, gather and dye discarded bird feathers.

❶ Glue feathers of the same color vertically in a band around the bottom portion of the lampshade, overlapping the edges.

❷ Glue a second band of differently colored feathers onto the lampshade, the tips overlapping the first band.

❸ Stick a final band of feathers onto the lampshade, applying glue along the upper rim. Cut the top of any longer feathers to align with the rim.

❹ Glue short feathers horizontally in a row around the upper rim, overlapping the ends.

Exotic Wall Hanging
Bunch together some colorful feathers and bind the ends tightly with colored yarn to make a stunning wall decoration. Snip the feather ends in bold zigzag patterns. The men of some Amazonian tribes sport nose-pins similar to this design.

CHAPTER TWO
BoDy and SouL

Zulu Speaking Beads

Morning Star Pendant • Hand of Fatima Amulet

All–Seeing Eye Symbols • Mola Appliqué Bag

Latvian Sun Belt

Patterns and Abstract Symbols

People have felt the need to protect themselves from the evils of life and beyond for centuries, using charms, amulets, and tattoos. The original safeguarding intent of these tokens has long been forgotten, and they are now often valued solely for their visual appeal. Specially designed for personal preservation and enhancement, here is a rich variety of decorative accessories to make and wear, inspired by traditional patterns and practices drawn from as far afield as South Africa and Central America. There is symbolically and brightly colored jewelry, including a bewitching, bejeweled amulet of Middle-Eastern origin, together with simple yet striking embroidered and hand-sewn items for the needleworker.

Zulu Speaking Beads

You will need

plain bangle
wax pencil
needle and thread
all-purpose household glue
rocaille beads in five colors
five brass buttons

The colorful beadwork of South African Zulus is a system of non-verbal communication. The patterns and colors have cultural and symbolic meanings, and can indicate social status when applied to clothes and jewelry or tokens of love.

Beads play an important part in coming-of-age and marriage ceremonies, marking the integration of the bride into the family of the groom. Small tokens are often added to the designs, such as wrapped candies, brass studs, or tiny bottles, to represent medicine and to ward off evil.

These bangles are inspired by the rope belts worn by unmarried Zulu women. Tribal clan colors are used, the colors representing various attributes. For example, pale blue means ripeness and fertility, black means depth and profundity, while white represents purity and innocence.

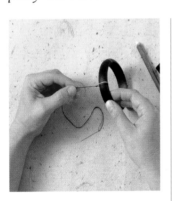

❶ To make the five-colored bangle, measure the outer circumference of the bangle and divide into five sections. Mark the divisions with the wax pencil. Thread a needle with a long length of thread, and knot the ends together. Loop the thread through the bangle, bringing the needle out between the threads. Pull tightly and glue the knot to the bangle at a division.

❷ Thread on a few beads of one color, then thread on a button so that it will be positioned in the center of the outer side. Continue threading on beads, wrapping them closely around the bangle as you work. When you have covered one section, change to another color, remembering to add a button at the dividing line.

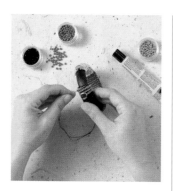

4 When the bangle is covered, thread the needle through the first four beads, then part the beads and glue the thread to the bangle. Cut off the excess thread. The shield bangle is worked in the same way, but divided into thirds instead of fifths. The shield is worked on one section, then the beads are counted and copied on the other sections.

3 If the thread runs out, cut off the needle and glue the thread ends to the bangle. Fasten a new length to the bangle as before, close to the last bead. Insert the needle through the last four beads before threading on more beads.

Beadwork Earrings

Glass rings for drapes have been wrapped with beads in the same way as the bangles to make these stunning earrings.

Morning Star Pendant

You will need

tracing paper

7-inch square of strong white
cotton fabric

dressmaker's carbon paper in
yellow

masking tape

ball-point pen

small glass beads in white,
red, yellow, turquoise, and
black

white silk sewing thread

straw (milliner's) needle size 7

small block of beeswax

two 2¹/₂-inch diameter circles
of thin card

scissors

fabric glue

4¹/₃-inch diameter circle of
red silk

gold-colored jump-ring

fine black leather thonging

Native American embroidered beadwork is outstanding for its use of symbols, which are the graphic expressions of the Indians' deep spiritual beliefs. Beadwork is used to decorate traditional dress and articles such as buckskin pouches, purses, and pendants. Animal and insect designs, all highly stylized, are widespread in bead embroidery, as are mountains, trails, and stars, particularly the morning star represented by a cross, but there are very few representations of plants and flowers. Many of the Indian tribes believed that natural phenomena were gods – the sun was the most powerful deity, followed by the moon, sky, earth, and wind.

Colors also have their symbolism, including red for blood, earth, and sunset; yellow for daylight and sunshine; green for plants and trees; blue for the wide expanse of the daytime sky; black for night. Many beadwork articles, especially pendants, are ornamented with fringes, feathers, shells, bells, and bear and elks' teeth.

This unusual pendant, featuring the morning star symbol, is made using a traditional Native American method of applying beads to cloth or buckskin. Called lazy squaw stitch, it is quick to work, since five beads are applied with every stitch.

❶ Trace off the full-size template on page 103. Place the white fabric on a flat surface and cover with a piece of carbon paper with the waxy side downward. Lay the tracing over the top and secure with strips of masking tape. Trace over the design with a ball-point pen.

❷ Using the photograph as a color guide, embroider the design with beads, using lazy squaw stitch (page 17.) To strengthen the thread, rub each length of thread across the block of beeswax several times before threading the needle.

❸ Lay the beadwork face downward on a flat surface. Position one card circle in the center. Cut away the surplus fabric, leaving a margin of about ³/₄ inch showing all round. Snip notches into the fabric and bring it forward over onto the back of the card. Stick in place with fabric glue. Repeat with the red silk and the other piece of card.

❹ To make the fringe, secure a length of waxed thread on the wrong side of the silk-covered circle, close to the edge. Turn the circle over so that the right side is facing you. Thread 10 yellow beads onto the needle, followed by 2 red and 4 white beads.

❻ Repeat steps 4 and 5 until you have made a section of fringe about 1¼ inches wide. Fasten off the thread end securely. Place the two circles together with wrong sides facing and the fringed section toward the bottom of the beaded design. Carefully oversew the two circles together, catching in a jump-ring at the top of the pendant. Thread the thonging through the jump-ring and knot the ends together.

❺ Push the beads up to the edge of the circle. Omitting the last white bead, insert the needle back through all the beads and into the fabric edge. Pull the thread through and gently tighten it. Bring the needle back to the front of the fabric close to the edge, ready to make the next fringe component.

Hand of Fatima Amulet

You will need

old scissors
tomato paste tube
craft knife
cutting-mat
kitchen paper towels
old ball-point pen
blue jewelry stone
superglue
two jump-rings
triangular pendant holder
blue-bead necklace

The evil eye represents jealousy and envy, and is an important symbol in all Mediterranean countries but especially in the Middle East (see opposite). Amulets are worn to ward off the evil eye, and protective symbols are painted onto buildings. The number five is evident in many of these defensive emblems.

Evil-eye amulets are often kept in spear-shaped pockets, since it is believed that the spear will pierce the eye and destroy its harmful effects.

The Hand of Fatima is a popular amulet to protect against evil. Fatima was the virtuous daughter of the Prophet Mohammed. This Hand of Fatima amulet is made from a tomato paste tube. The inside is a rich golden color, and can be easily embossed. Suspend the amulet from a blue-bead necklace — blue beads are believed to have protective qualities in Mediterranean countries. The jewelry findings can be bought from craft stores or mail order suppliers.

❶ Using an old pair of scissors, cut open a tomato paste tube. Remove the contents and store in an airtight container for future use. Wash and dry the tube. Use the template on page 103 to draw the amulet on the outer side of the tube.

❷ Using the scissors, cut out the basic shape of the amulet, then cut out the intricate areas between the fingers with a craft knife while resting on a cutting-mat.

❸ Place the amulet face down on a double thickness of kitchen paper towel. Pierce a hole at the dot with a the tip of a scissor blade. Draw the decorative design on the amulet with an old ball-point pen to emboss the metal, leaving a space at the center bottom for the jewelry stone.

❹ Glue the jewelry stone onto the right side of the amulet. Fix a jump-ring to the hole, then fix another ring to the first one.

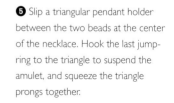

❺ Slip a triangular pendant holder between the two beads at the center of the necklace. Hook the last jump-ring to the triangle to suspend the amulet, and squeeze the triangle prongs together.

All-seeing Eye Symbols

The all-seeing eye is often regarded as a path for wisdom and enlightenment that links the outer material world and the inner spiritual life. It can also be a conduit for darker forces, such as the evil eye that transmits curses and bad luck with one glance.

Medusa

The Greek goddess Medusa was transformed from a great beauty to an old hag with snakes for hair after making love in the temple of Athene. A single look from Medusa would turn a man to stone, and her head appears on weapons as a symbol of fear.

Sailor's Talisman

Eyes are painted on boats throughout the world to guide them safely through waters. Mediterranean fishermen have painted eyes on the bows of their boats for centuries; the eyes are believed to "see" their way to the richest hauls of fish.

Eye of Horus

Wedjat, or the Eye of Horus, was a sacred magical symbol in ancient Egypt. The eye represents the omnipresent sky god, Horus, the right eye being the sun and the left eye, the moon.

Eye of Wisdom

An almond shape containing one circle inside another is an Islamic symbol. The eye transports the outside world to its inner spiritual center, which is represented by the smaller circle, via the outer circle, which is the soul.

Mola Appliqué Bag

You will need

tracing paper

¹/₄ yard of 36-inch wide red fabric

¹/₄ yard of 36-inch wide yellow fabric

¹/₂ yard of 36-inch wide blue fabric

¹/₄ yard of 36-inch wide green fabric

wax pencil

dressmaking pins

needle and thread

bodkin

five yellow buttons

two small tassels

The Cuna Indians of the San Blas islands of Panama believe that every creature and plant has a spirit, and that they can be protected from evil by drawing an image of these spirits on their bodies with tattoos or paint. The Cunas have no written language, so this imagery is used in picture writing.

The vibrant designs of mola (literally meaning clothing) appliqué are derived from these forms of body decoration. Today, the Cunas decorate fabric panels to be applied to blouses with this form of reverse appliqué. Two or more layers of contrasting colored fabrics are layered together. The top layer is cut away in a series of contoured lines to form abstract patterns, animals, birds, and plants. The Tree of Life and Mother Earth are popular symbols. The cut edges are turned under and slipstitched to the lower layers.

❶ Trace the template on page 102 and cut out the sections. Cut one rectangle of red fabric and two of yellow fabric 12 × 6¹/₄ inches. Matching the upper edges, draw around the tracing on the red rectangle using the wax pencil. Pin the red rectangle to one yellow rectangle. Tack together around the design.

❷ Using sharp embroidery scissors, cut through the top layer between the outlines. Snip the curves. Turn the raw edges under along the outlines and slipstitch to the yellow fabric using tiny stitches.

❸ Cut a bias strip of blue fabric 8 × 1 inches for button loops and 16¹/₂ × 1¹/₂ inches for a handle. Stitch the long edges, taking a 1/4-inch seam allowance. Turn right side out with a bodkin.

❹ Cut the button loops into three suitable lengths and stitch to the unembroidered end of the red rectangle. Pin the remaining yellow rectangle on top as a lining. Stitch across the ends of the rectangle, taking a ³/₈-inch seam allowance. Turn right side out.

❺ Fold the bag in half, red side outward. For the bindings, cut two bias strips of green fabric 6¹/₄ × 2³/₄ inches and press lengthwise in half. With right sides facing and taking a ³/₈-inch seam allowance, stitch the bindings to the raw edges of the bag with the ends extending.

❻ Turn the ends under, then slipstitch the pressed edge to the back of the bag. Turn in the ends of the handle and handsew. Fasten the bag with three buttons. Sew a tassel at the bottom of the bindings, then sew a button above.

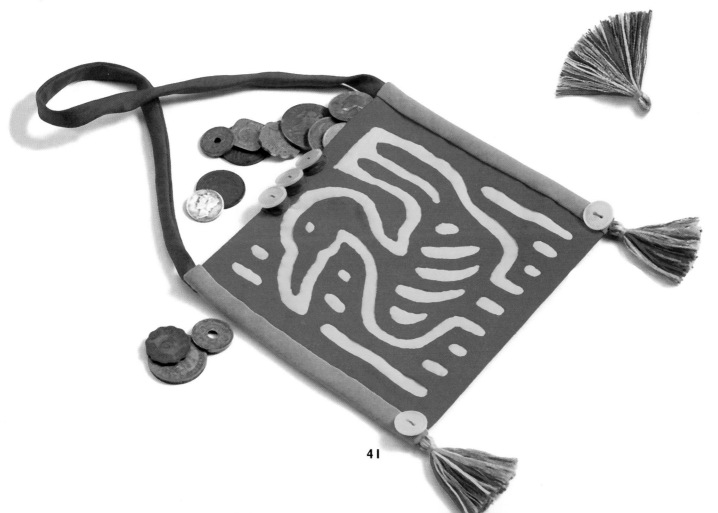

Latvian Sun Belt

You will need

4-inch wide strip of white 11-count Aida long enough to fit around your waist, plus 6 inches for overlap

3¼-inch wide strip of red felt, 2½ inches longer than the finished belt

1¼ yards of 2-inch wide belt backing

DMC stranded cotton in red 666, blue 791, yellow 444, green 909, and light green 703

needlepoint needle size 24

iron

tacking thread and sewing needle

white sewing thread and pins

pinking shears

belt buckle

Latvia, on the eastern shore of the Baltic Sea, is a country whose artistic traditions are steeped in folklore. Latvian people have a strong cultural heritage, shown in the 36,000 dainas or folk songs that have been written down and preserved since the late 1800s. These dainas provide details of Latvia's daily and ceremonial life and customs, and are particularly rich in references to knitting. Intricately patterned mittens have been knitted for many hundreds of years and are still important today, especially during the rites of marriage when a young woman can prove her worth as a future bride and homemaker by the quality of the mittens she knits for her bridal chest.

The chief colors used in Latvian knitting are red, blue, green, and yellow. All the designs are geometric and most are deeply symbolic. The sun, the yellow motif on the belt, is often depicted as a powerful woman, and the green motifs portray Usins, the driver of the sun's carriage in her journey across the sky who enables her to return in the spring. The zigzag blue border edging the belt depicts Mara who protects cattle and the purity of the drinking water.

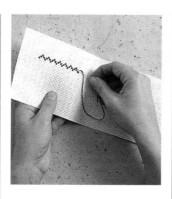

❶ Measure your waist and add 6 inches to this measurement for overlap and turnings. Cut a piece of Aida to this length and 4 inches wide. Cut the felt and belt backing to size.

❷ Beginning 1¼ inches from the raw edge at one end of the fabric and positioning the design centrally along the strip, work the repeating design from the chart (page 106) in cross stitch (page 17), using three strands of thread in the needlepoint needle. Each colored square represents one complete cross stitch. Continue working the repeats until you are 1¼ inches from the opposite end of the strip.

❸ Press the embroidery lightly on the wrong side with a warm iron. Place the embroidery face downward on a flat surface and lay the belt backing centrally over the top. Turn the raw edges of the fabric over the backing and tack in place all round the edge.

❹ Place the felt strip on a flat surface and pin the embroidery over the top so that an even margin of felt shows along each edge. Machine-stitch close to the edge through all the layers. Trim the felt with pinking shears to make a decorative edge. Insert one end of the belt through the buckle, fold over, and stitch securely in place.

Patterns and Abstract Symbols

Over time, many figurative motifs have become simplified into abstract patterns. Designing with abstract shapes and patterns is ideal for those who are not confident at drawing more realistic, representational forms.

The Sri Yantra
The intricate geometric patterns of the Sri Yantra depict the universe and its gods. The Sri Yantra is used in meditation as a visual focus, to help the mind concentrate on the act of creation of the universe.

Square
The square represents many positive attributes, including honesty and safety. In Hinduism, it is associated with order. A simple motif set inside a square has a bold elegance.

Lozenge
To Native North Americans, the lozenge or diamond represented the medicine man's eye and meant vigilance and wisdom. It is a form of the "yoni" in the East, and often appears in Tantric iconography.
In Western magic, the lozenge stands for volatility.

The Maze
In many cultures, the maze represents an inner journey of the mind through confusion and indecision. A maze would be an excellent motif to work in cross stitch or tent stitch needlepoint.

Seal of Solomon

These interwoven triangles were the sacred seal of King Solomon of Israel. The Hebrew symbol represents the everlasting union of heaven and earth. It is often worn as an evil-eye amulet.

Pentagram

The five triangular sections of the five-pointed star denote the four elements, together with spirituality. It was used as a symbolic figure by the Pythagoreans, the brotherhood founded by the Ancient Greek mathematician, Pythagoras.

Downward-Pointing Triangle

A downward-pointing triangle denotes the moon and feminine creativity. When blue, it stands for water and is connected with the astrological water sign, Scorpio. When green, the triangle represents earth and is associated with the earth sign, Taurus.

Swastika

The four spokes of the swastika represent the four levels of existence to the Jains. Generally, the swastika means good luck, health, and prosperity. It is often painted on the threshold of houses in India to ward off evil. Be sure to use the clockwise spinning form, which has positive qualities.

Upward-Pointing Triangle

Pointing toward the heavens, the triangle symbolizes the rising sun and divine attainment. A red triangle represents fire and a gold triangle denotes the air. This symbol would be effective as a hand-painted motif on a silk scarf or handkerchief.

CHAPTER THREE
FroM the EarTh

Spirit Skeleton

Navaho Sand Painting Scarf

Sacred Scarab Box   *Egyptian Hieroglyphics*

Ganesha Wall Plaque   *Aromatic Bay Tree*

Tree Symbols   *Inca Coffee Cups*

Our ancestors relied directly on the earth to provide the basic essentials for everyday living. They tended crops for food and to supply materials for building and furnishing their homes. These resources, being natural, returned to where they came from after having served their useful purpose, thereby continuing the cycle of life. Rituals are still performed the world over to thank the gods for these invaluable gifts. In this chapter, clay formed from the most basic of the elements — water and the life-giving earth — is made into enchanting and entertaining models; the beautiful, healing paintings drawn in sand by the Navahos have been translated into a stunning silk scarf, and ancient Peruvian pottery designs are used to ornament contemporary china.

Spirit Skeleton

You will need

air-drying clay
thick wire
knife
thick needle
rolling pin
paintbrush
craft paints
thick thread

Mexicans celebrate the Christian festival of the Day of the Dead on November 2. The festival is derived from ancient Aztec religious ceremonies involving skulls and masks. The favorite foods of recently departed loved ones are displayed on altars in the home. Clay and papier mâché death figures are used to decorate the altars along with edible effigies of skulls and graves.

Trails of yellow petals (yellow being the ancient color of death) are laid from the house to the cemetery, to lead the spirits back after they have visited their relatives' homes.

This weird guy is fashioned from clay, then boldly painted. The limbs are modeled separately and attached with thread, to give the figure an amusing stance.

❶ Roll a ball of clay 1¼ inches in diameter, and mold it into a pear shape for the skull. Pull the narrow end forward for the chin. Press either side of the center of the skull to indent the eye sockets.

❷ Roll a ball of clay 1¾ inches in diameter. Mold to an oval and flatten slightly for the body. Push the ends of a piece of wire 1½ inches long into the skull and body to form a neck.

❸ Cut a "V" out of either side of the body to separate the rib cage from the pelvis. Flatten slightly across the division, then pat the cut edges with a moistened finger to create a more rounded shape.

❹ Wrap clay around the wire "neck." Blend onto the skull and body with a moistened finger.

❺ Roll two "fingers" of clay ½ inch thick and 4¾ inches long for the legs, and two "fingers" ⅜ inch thick and 3¾ inch long for arms. Round the ends of each limb.

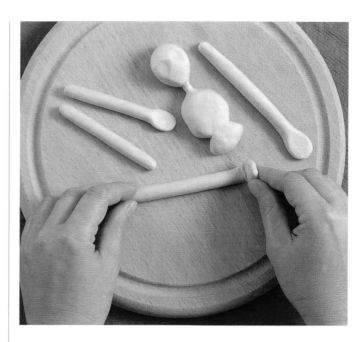

❻ Flatten one end of each limb to make feet and hands. Bend the feet upward.

❼ Arrange the limbs appropriately against the skeleton. Make holes through the pelvis and top of the legs with a needle so that they can be joined together.

❽ Make a hole through the rib cage, then through the top of the arms from side to side so that they can be joined together.

9 Mold a conical shape for the hat crown. Moisten, and press to the top of the skull. Make a hole at the top of the hat crown for hanging. Roll out a piece of clay ⁵/₃₂ inch thick, and cut a crescent shape for the hat brim and a rectangle 2¹/₂ × ³/₄ inch for the blanket.

10 Moisten the underside and press the hat brim over the crown and the blanket across the body. Leave the pieces to dry.

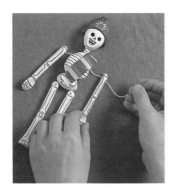

11 Paint the model. Tie the legs to the pelvis with thick thread, knotting the ends together at the back of the figure. Thread a needle with thick thread and insert through the arms and rib cage. Knot the thread ends, securing the arms against the body. Suspend the skeleton on a thread.

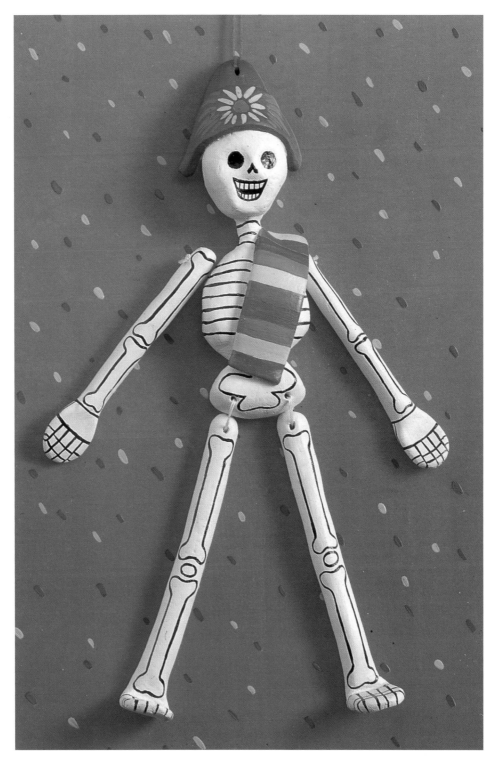

Navaho Sand Painting Scarf

You will need

20-inch square of cream
  Habotai silk
masking tape
pencil or fade-away
  embroidery marker
silk-painting or batik frame
3-point silk pins
metallic copper outliner
outliner bottle with fine nib
iron-fix silk paints in red,
  yellow, black, blue-gray
cotton buds
opaque white fabric paint
fine paint brush
white tissue paper
iron
cream silk sewing thread
sewing needle

The Navaho are a semi-nomadic Native American nation living in reservations in northern Arizona, northwestern New Mexico, and southern Utah. The Navaho create beautiful sand paintings which form an important part of their culture. The paintings are destroyed as soon as they are completed because the act of creation is more important spiritually than the finished product. Creating a sand painting contributes to the Navaho idea of harmony — the hozho. Literally translated as "beauty," hozho actually means more than that. The word refers to the environment, to harmony, happiness, and everything in life that is positive. Life for the Navaho is a constant attempt to create, enhance, and live in hozho and, after death, to join the hozho that permeates the universe.

The paintings are made by both ordinary Navaho men and by medicine men or healers in an effort to cure a sick person. A thick layer of sand is spread on the floor, then smoothed with a curved stick. The painter works from the center of the sand, taking a pinch of the desired color and trickling it onto the smooth background.

This luxurious silk scarf portrays a Navaho design called "Red Antway", which is painted in the symbolic colors of red, yellow, black, blue-gray, and white.

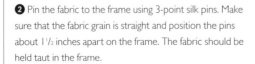

❶ Enlarge the template on page 105 to fit, leaving a margin of 2 inches. Cover with the pressed silk and secure with tape. Transfer the design with a pencil or the marker.

❷ Pin the fabric to the frame using 3-point silk pins. Make sure that the fabric grain is straight and position the pins about 1½ inches apart on the frame. The fabric should be held taut in the frame.

❸ Stir the outliner thoroughly and transfer to the outliner bottle. Squeeze the bottle gently over scrap paper until the outliner flows evenly through the nib. Starting at the center and touching the nib to the fabric, apply the outliner in a continuous line.

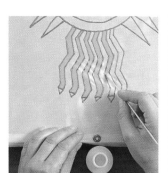

4 Allow the outliner to dry completely – this may take several hours. Stir the silk paint vigorously. Using the photograph as a color guide, apply the first color. Soak a cotton bud in paint, then press it onto the fabric, and allow the paint to flood across the outlined shape. Add more paint until the shape is filled.

5 Leave the first color to dry, then apply the remaining colors in the same way, making sure you allow each color to dry before proceeding to the next. Stir the white fabric paint thoroughly, then carefully apply it to the white areas of the design using a fine paintbrush.

6 Leave to dry for at least 48 hours. To fix the colors, sandwich the silk right side downward between white tissue paper, and press with a hot iron for two minutes. Rinse the silk in cold water, allow to dry, then press on the wrong side with a cool iron. Turn a narrow hem around the edge and secure with hand-stitching.

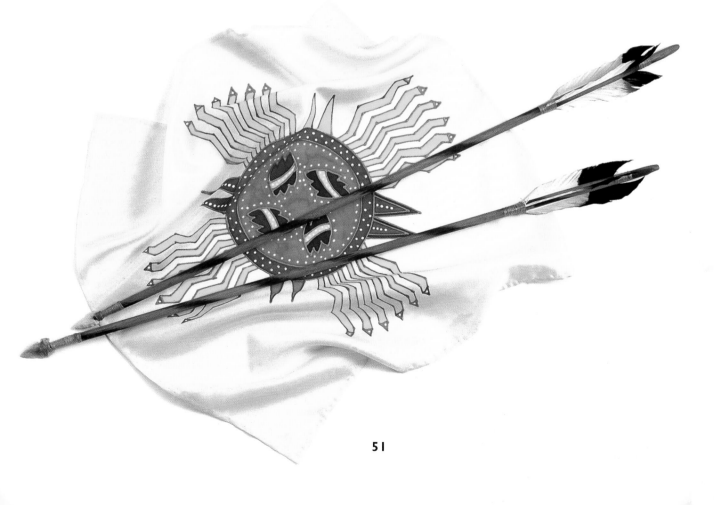

You will need

air-drying clay
small knife
box
superglue
craft paints
paintbrushes

Sacred Scarab Box

The humble dung beetle became a sacred creature to the people of ancient Egypt, possessing special powers. The beetle lays its eggs in a nest of dung, which it rolls along in front of it. To the Egyptians, this ball of new life reminded them of the sun. They imagined that the sun was pushed across the sky, like a giant ball filled with new life, by a mighty scarab. Every day the scarab pushed the sun across the sky, from dawn until dusk. It came to symbolize the joy of renewal, fertility, and the endurance of the human soul. The Egyptians wore scarab amulets to protect them in life and to go with them into their tombs, to win favor with the sun-god.

This handsome box is a reminder of the charming tale of the beetle that pushes the sun across the sky, and as a symbol of renewal, it will perhaps bring a fresh start and a change of fortune to its owner.

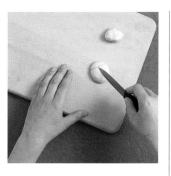

❶ Mold a 1¼-inch diameter ball of clay into an oval and slightly flatten it. With a knife, indent a line across the oval to define the head, leaning the blade to one side and then the other. Indent another line to divide the body in half.

❷ Indent a "V" on the body sections. Roll two small ovals of clay. Moisten and press to each end of the scarab. Divide the oval on the head into three sections with the knife. Press a small piece of moistened clay against the oval and cut into four points, pulling away the excess clay.

❸ To make the legs, roll six cylinders of clay ¼ inch thick. Cut to ¾ inch in length. Squeeze the ends to round them. Moisten and press to the sides of the scarab. Indent lines on the legs with the knife.

Alternatively, make a scarab from terracotta clay and glue a fastening-pin onto the underside. Apply a coat of matte varnish for protection.

❹ Leave to dry, then glue to the box lid. Paint the box and scarab. Paint hieroglyphics as a border on the lid.

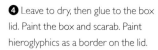

Egyptian Hieroglyphics

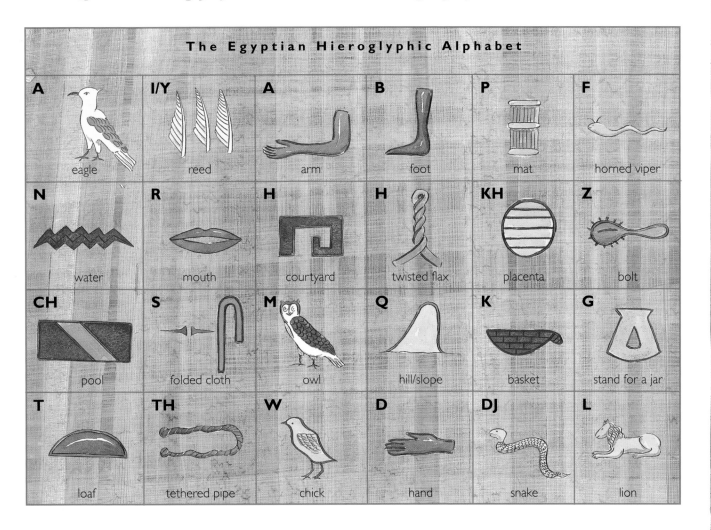

The Egyptian Hieroglyphic Alphabet

A		I/Y		A		B		P		F	
eagle		reed		arm		foot		mat		horned viper	
N		**R**		**H**		**H**		**KH**		**Z**	
water		mouth		courtyard		twisted flax		placenta		bolt	
CH		**S**		**M**		**Q**		**K**		**G**	
pool		folded cloth		owl		hill/slope		basket		stand for a jar	
T		**TH**		**W**		**D**		**DJ**		**L**	
loaf		tethered pipe		chick		hand		snake		lion	

The ancient Egyptians used all kinds of sacred symbols to decorate everything from boxes and brooches to the tombs of god-kings, such as the famous Tutankhamun. Even shapes had meanings – the pyramids, for example, which represent the highest spiritual attainment.

The Ancient Egyptian language of hieroglyphics uses pictures of objects with recognizable meanings, and words that sound like their meanings. The script was sacred, and today we can understand much about the beliefs of the ancient Egyptians through their beautiful hieroglyphics.

We can use the symbolic shapes and picture language of hieroglyphics to add a little extra meaning to crafts we make today. Using the alphabet above, you can personalize your scarab by drawing a person's name in pictures, or adding a special, mystical message to the box.

Ganesha Wall Plaque

You will need

air-drying terra-cotta clay
wooden chopping board
rolling pin
small sharp knife
plastic drinking straw
dressmaking pin

Ganesha, the benevolent elephant-headed Hindu god, represents sacred wisdom and prudence. Revered as the scribe who wrote the Mahabharata, Ganesha is traditionally portrayed upright, and offering gifts and protection.

Plaques depicting Ganesha are made of clay and donkey dung by the potters of southern Rajasthan in India for the harvest celebrations in January and February. This appealing wall plaque is modeled from air-drying terra-cotta clay.

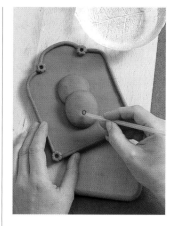

5 Roll a ball of clay 1½ inches in diameter for the head. Mold into an oval and flatten slightly. Pull, then roll one half into a cylindrical shape for the trunk. Moisten the underside of the head and arrange in place on the plaque. Tip the trunk tip upward.

2 Roll four balls of clay ⅜ inch in diameter for the flowers, and flatten slightly. Hold the knife upright and cut into the sides to form six petals. Moisten the underside and press onto each corner of the plaque. Punch a hole through the center of each flower with a drinking straw so that the plaque can be hung.

3 Roll a ball of clay 1¼ inches in diameter for the chest and a ball 1½ inches in diameter for the stomach. Mold the stomach into an oval. Flatten both pieces to ⅜ inch thick.

4 Moisten the undersides and press the chest to the center of the plaque. Press the stomach to the plaque, overlapping the chest. Press the end of the straw into the stomach to suggest a navel.

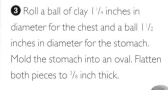

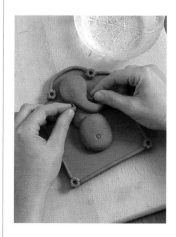

1 Roll the clay out flat on a wooden chopping board to a thickness of 5/16 inch, and cut a rectangle 6 x 4¾ inches. Cut three scallops along the top edge of the rectangle, and pull away the excess clay. Roll a clay cylinder ¼ inch thick, moisten, and arrange around the edges. The clay cylinder can be cut and joined at the corners of the plaque.

6 Roll two small tapering cylinders for tusks and bend in a curve. Cut the wide ends diagonally, moisten, and press to each side of the trunk. Smooth the tusks to the head with a moistened finger. "Draw" the eyes and make a pattern along the trunk with the knife tip. Indent the eyeballs with the head of a dressmaking pin.

7 Roll some clay out flat to a wafer thinness, and cut an oval for the ears 1¼ inches long. Cut the oval lengthwise in half, moisten the undersides, and slip the ears under the head at each side.

8 Roll cylinders of clay ½ inch thick and cut into six 2-inch lengths for limbs. Cut one end of each limb diagonally. Press two to each side of the chest. Tip the ends outward. Position the remaining pieces as legs.

9 Model gifts and decorations from clay, moisten the undersides, and press to the model. Use the knife-tip and pin-head to add details. Set aside to harden overnight.

Aromatic Bay Tree

You will need

terra-cotta plant pot
all-purpose household glue
dried thyme
knife
dry florist's foam block
dry florist's foam cone
wooden stick
bay leaves
reindeer moss

The ancient Greeks and Romans regarded the bay tree (Laurus Nobilis) as sacred. They worked the leaves into wreaths and garlands to celebrate their victories and crown their favorite poets, hence the title "poet laureate." Bay leaves have many medicinal applications, and were traditionally believed to ward off witches and lightning.

This charming tree stands in a pot covered with aromatic dried thyme. Thyme denotes activity and purity in some cultures. In others, it stands for such desirable qualities as courage, longevity, and good health.

❶ Spread glue onto a section of the plant pot and sprinkle dried thyme on top. Continue until the pot is covered, leaving the rim free of thyme. Shake off the excess.

❷ Cut the foam block to fit inside the pot. Dab with glue and wedge the block inside the pot. Insert the stick upright in the center of the foam. Press the foam cone onto the top of the stick.

❸ Starting at the base, glue bay leaves in rows around the cone, overlapping the leaves. Continue to the top of the cone, covering the foam completely. Glue moss onto the top of the foam in the pot.

Tree Symbols

The Tree of Life is an emblem of perfect harmony. The fruit it bears represents many virtues —
wisdom, truth, and love, for example. Trees appear in symbolic forms throughout the world.
Many are thought to have healing properties, and some are worshipped. A forest of trees
symbolizes mystery and transformation.

The Peach Tree

In China, peaches are associated with marriage and long life. The Chinese god of long life, Shou-lao, is often shown with a peach from a tree that bears fruits once every 3,000 years in the gardens of Paradise. The ancient Chinese believed that trees close to tombs were imbued with the spirits of the dead.

The Hawthorn Tree

A green sprig from a hawthorn tree was believed to ward off naughty fairies on the eve of May Day, but it had to be without the white may blossom, which was thought to entice death. Even today, many people will not allow may flowers in the home.

The Oak Tree

For the Celts and early Druids, the oak stood for divinity and masculinity. It was also held in great esteem by the Norse people. Travelers avoided passing through a plantation of oak trees at night, since it was believed that the spirits of felled oak trees took revenge on mortal beings.

The World Tree

The roots of the World Tree encircle the entire world, and its branches reach the heavens. It represents the power of mankind to reach spirituality.

The Green Man

The representation of the tree as a man is a Western symbol of fertility, depicting masculine energy impregnating the earth with new life. Willows were thought to resemble man and amble about at night, frightening lone travelers. Traditionally, the Green Man represented the regenerative force of Christ.

Inca Coffee Cups

You will need

white china coffee cups and
    saucers
soft pencil
ceramic paints
paintbrushes
cotton bud and white spirit
    (optional)
soft cloth

Much of the pottery of the pre-Columbians of South America was decorated with magic and religious motifs. The ancient Nazca pottery of Peru was embellished with supernatural cat-like creatures. The Moche peoples of northern Peru painted detailed characters of religious significance on their pottery. They also modeled erotic clay figures, which are thought to have denoted fertility.

The Incas of Peru were fine ceramicists, and decorated their wares with geometric patterns that may have represented the patterning on animal skins. These often appear on arybolas – traditional vessels for carrying "chicha," a fermented corn beer. These coffee cups and saucers are painted with Inca motifs using ceramic paints.

❶ Draw a geometric motif onto the cup and four motifs onto the saucer, or draw a simple character within a square on the cup and mark a border on the saucer. Keep the designs on the cup ³/₄ inch below the upper edge.

❷ Paint the designs. Work a section at a time with the cups facing upward so that the paint does not run. Any mistakes can be wiped away with a cotton bud dipped in white spirit. Allow to dry.

3 Outline the designs and add details with black paint, using a fine paintbrush. Buff the china with a soft cloth when the paint has dried, to remove any traces of pencil. The china can be washed in warm, soapy water.

This striking geometric motif is of typical Inca design.

CHAPTER FOUR
BLeSS THiS HouSe

Evergreen Fortune Garland
Flower Symbols   *Harvest Corn Dolly*
Indian Welcome Mat
Rooster Weather Vane
Huichol Bead Bowl

The need people have to honor homes with gifts and votives is universal. Lucky and protective symbols are often painted at the threshold of dwelling places. Housewarming parties and gifts to make a new house a home are prevalent in modern societies, while the completion of new buildings is marked by a variety of ceremonies. The following projects offer a range of decorative ideas for adorning the home, to bring good fortune and protection to family and friends within. A garland will bring festive cheer to visitors, while a floorcloth painted with a sacred, stylized Indian design offers a lasting welcome. An intricately woven corn dolly sustains the warmth of high summer through winter months, and a Mexican-inspired beaded bowl offers a kaleidoscope of uplifting, spiritual motifs.

Evergreen Fortune Garland

You will need

gold card
cutting-mat
craft knife
steel ruler
masking tape
fine wire
florist's wet foam ring
sprays of cypress, holly, and
   ivy
artificial red berries

Evergreen trees universally represent longevity. To the Scandinavians, they symbolized the eternal life force, and featured in their winter solstice festivities. The Romans celebrated the goddess Sternia with evergreen boughs, and pagans believed that evergreens brought good fortune because they kept their leaves in the fall.

Holly is thought to ward off witches and denotes the male, and to Christians its red berries represent Christ's blood. Ivy is regarded as female, and stands for friendship and consistency because it clings tightly. It was sacred to Osiris, the Egyptian god, and Dionysos, the Greek god. Ivy is also associated with Bacchus, the god of wine, and was thought to protect against drunkenness.

Evergreen garlands have featured in Christmas festivities for hundreds of years. The circular garland was thought to bring good luck. Hung on a door, this festive wreath would offer a warm welcome to your guests at Christmas.

❶ Working on a cutting-mat, cut out lots of stars from gold card using a craft knife and steel ruler. Stick a length of fine wire to the backs of the stars with masking tape.

❷ Soak the ring in water. Insert sprigs of cypress into the ring, working in the same direction. When the foam is covered, add sprigs of holly and ivy around the ring in the same way.

❸ Insert the stars at random into the ring, bending the wires so that the stars face upward. Add the artificial berries at intervals in any remaining gaps around the ring.

Flower Symbols

Flowers are often associated with feminine beauty. The ancient Chinese believed that a flower bloomed in the next world for every woman living. A bud represents creation and the power of the sun, and flowers symbolize not only youth but also fragility. The plant world symbolizes the cycle of life — fertility, death, and rebirth. Many flowers and herbs are thought to have magical and healing powers.

Marigold

Often an omen, marigolds predict the need to be wary of the future. In Mexico, they represent death and feature in the Day of the Dead festival.

Geranium

Geraniums are traditionally chosen for wedding bouquets. An oak-leafed geranium signifies true friendship, and a silver-leafed variety assures well-being.

Honeysuckle

Honeysuckle represents the bonds of love because it entwines itself around other flowers. It is also associated with heightening passion and desire.

Clover

The four-leafed clover is considered lucky because of its rarity; it also signifies love returned. It is also a sign that the finder will meet his or her future love.

Lotus

Because it grows from within a pond and becomes a beautiful flower, the lotus represents a soul rising from confusion to clarity. It is connected with the sun and moon in the East, and regarded as the flower of Aphrodite in the West. In the traditional European language of flowers, a lotus flower signifies estranged love.

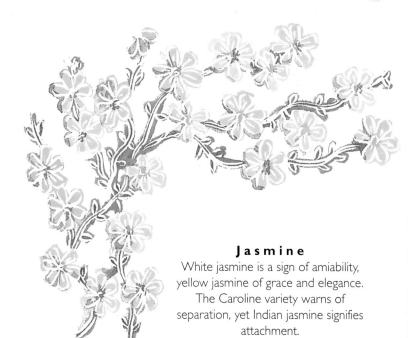

Rose

Red buds are a sign of purity and love, but a deep red flower means shame and bashfulness. A white rose means youth and innocence, and a yellow rose represents rejected love.

Jasmine

White jasmine is a sign of amiability, yellow jasmine of grace and elegance. The Caroline variety warns of separation, yet Indian jasmine signifies attachment.

Daffodil

The Celts believed that daffodils would make their livestock infertile. Farmers banned them in case the eggs of their ducks and chickens failed to hatch.

Sunflower

As a symbol of the sun, the sunflower was worshipped by the Incas and the Native Americans. A dwarf sunflower denotes adoration.

Tulip

Red tulips signify love, but yellow tulips communicate hopeless love. Variegated tulips were traditionally given to those possessing beautiful eyes.

Harvest Corn Dolly

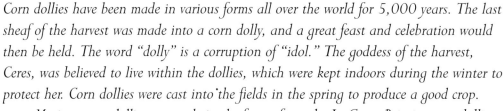

You will need

five stalks of wheat
bleach (optional)
thread
scissors
ribbon

Corn dollies have been made in various forms all over the world for 5,000 years. The last sheaf of the harvest was made into a corn dolly, and a great feast and celebration would then be held. The word "dolly" is a corruption of "idol." The goddess of the harvest, Ceres, was believed to live within the dollies, which were kept indoors during the winter to protect her. Corn dollies were cast into the fields in the spring to produce a good crop.

Mexican corn dollies are made in the form of angels. In Great Britain, corn dollies take the form of lanterns in Norfolk, Yorkshire, and Herefordshire, spirals in Essex, and fans in Wales.

Farmhands made five-straw favors, similar to this example, as love tokens for their sweethearts. Finish the dolly with a ribbon bow — red represents warmth and poppies, green symbolizes fertility and the spring, whereas blue exemplifies truth and cornflowers.

❷ Tie the straws together firmly below the ears.

❹ Fold the third straw anti-clockwise over the next two straws. Repeat with the fifth straw, then continue the sequence to the end of the stalks.

❶ Cut through the wheat stalks just above the first joint. Strip away the outer leaves. Soak the wheat in warm water until it is pliable, but try to avoid soaking the ears. A little bleach in the water will discourage mildew.

❸ Fold the first straw anti-clockwise over the next two.straws.

❺ Bend the braid into a loop and tie the ends behind the ears. Cut off any excess straw. Tie ribbon in a bow around the fastening.

Corn Stook Vase

Sheaves of corn represent the fertility of the earth and of the inner mind. This charming pot resembles a rustic stook of cereal crops. Simply slip an elastic band over a washed tin can. Slide crops and grasses diagonally behind the band to hide the can, then trim the ends level with the lower edge. Fasten a length of twine around the can, and cut away the elastic band.

67

Indian Welcome Mat

Each year, the outside walls of homes throughout India are decoratively painted in accordance with tribal tradition. Many of the paintings are sacred and mark the changing seasons. Women in Madhubani daub a preparation of rice paste onto the floors to conjure up the protection of gods.

In Western Rajasthan, images of the life-giving sun or lucky parrots are applied with whitewash over the doorways of the houses. Symbolic decorations known as "mandana" are applied daily to the thresholds during festivals, using colored paints. The mandana records the family's achievements and aspirations. Washed away by the annual monsoon, the mandana is recreated every year.

This practical, painted floor cloth is influenced by a traditional mandana depicting the Tree of Life. A few coats of varnish will protect it and make it a lasting welcome to your guests when placed at the threshold of your home.

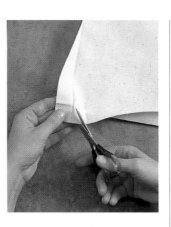

❶ Cut a rectangle of canvas for the floor cloth, allowing 1 inch on all sides for the hem. The finished size of this example measures 39 x 28 inches. Press the hem edges underneath, open them out at the corner, and cut diagonally across the corners to form miters.

❷ Refold the hem and glue neatly in place with all-purpose household glue. Apply three coats of primer or latex paint to the top surface. Allow to dry between coats, then sand lightly.

❸ Referring to the photograph, use a pencil to draw the design lightly onto the canvas. Alternatively, create your own pattern. It is not necessary to draw in all the details – keep the design simple.

❹ Paint the main colors of the border, then the tree and the background. Leave to dry, then fill in the finer details.

❺ When the paint has dried, apply three coats of varnish.

Rooster Weather Vane

Weather vanes were originally religious symbols. The rooster was a popular emblem because of its links with the crowing cockerel in the Bible. Many churches have biblical weather vanes as a sign of Christianity. In the first century AD, Andronicus built a magnificent bronze weather vane in Athens. The Vikings put wind indicators to practical use on their great ships. In more recent times, farmers in Western countries fashioned animal-shaped weather vanes from metal or wood to ward off bad luck.

This stylish ornamental model is made from fine copper. Contact with the air corrodes the surface of many metals, and causes an attractive patination known as verdigris. Realistic verdigris effects are reproduced here with household paints.

❶ Use the template on page 104 to cut the rooster from a sheet of fine copper using an old pair of scissors – the metal will blunt the blades. Pierce a hole at the dot for the eye with a push-pin. Enlarge the hole by pushing through the tips of the scissor blades.

❷ Paint the rooster and dowel with pale aquamarine paint as an undercoat, and leave to dry. Apply the two shades of aquamarine paint and viridian designer's gouache to the rooster and dowel, blending the colors together on the surface.

❸ Leave to dry, then gently rub with wire wool to reveal the undercoat and even the copper in places.

❹ Dilute burnt umber watercolor paint and apply to the surface to age the paint effect. Leave to dry, then apply a coat of polyurethane matte varnish for protection.

5 Place the dowel under the position of the remaining dots on the rooster, with the dowel extending below the metal. Carefully hammer a push-pin through each hole.

6 Color the natural wood with wood stain if you wish. Drill a hole through the center of the wood to fit the diameter of the dowel. Stand the length of dowel upright in the hole and glue in position.

Huichol Bead Bowl

You will need

small shallow bowl
wax pencil
all-purpose household glue
pair of tweezers
plastic rocaille beads

The Huichol (pronounced witch-ol) people of the Sierra Madre Occidental of Mexico are thought to be descended from the Aztecs. They create beautiful embroidery, yarn paintings, and beadwork. The symbolic images that appear in their art come from their use of peyote, a hallucinogenic cactus that reveals the secrets of the universe. Each embroidered stitch or bead denotes a seed that will flower or bear fruit and pass on religious knowledge to future generations.

Peyote mandalas take the form of kaleidoscopic designs in yarn paintings and on masks and bowls. These mandalas are the entrance to the spirit world. The sun, moon, animals, birds, and plants also feature in these works of art. This brightly colored bowl is inspired by the colorful containers fashioned from gourds that are left as offerings at ceremonial sites. The beads would traditionally be applied with beeswax.

❶ Using a wax pencil, mark the center of the bowl with a cross, then draw a simple design inside the bowl with a motif in the middle.

❷ Spread a little glue in the center of the bowl. Starting at the center of the cross, stick a bead in place using the tweezers, then build up the central motif with other beads, radiating outward.

❸ Continue to cover the entire surface of the bowl in a pattern of beads, applying a small amount of glue at a time so that it does not dry out. Add a patterned border around the rim.

CHAPTER FIVE
A Stitch in Time

Mien Jewelry Purse
Mexican Star Weaving
Indonesian Batik Cushion Cover
Magical Animals and Mythical Beasts
Caucasian Rug Pincushion

Many cultures have a rich heritage of needlecraft. With no written language, stories of creation and ancestry were told by needle and thread. Fortunately, many of these works have survived the centuries, and from them we can learn much about the folklore of remote areas of the world. This chapter reveals a diverse range of exquisite textile designs that have stood, and will continue to stand, the test of time, from a cross-stitched embroidered jewelry purse, inspired by the traditional motifs of the Mien people of northern Thailand, and brilliantly colored Latin American-style star-shaped yarn weavings, through to a fresh, contemporary adaptation of a Javanese batik pattern and a needlepoint pincushion, fashioned after the fabulous geometric designs of the Caucasian rug-weavers.

Mien Jewelry Purse

You will need

two 11-inch squares of white
  11-count Aida
old newspapers and clear
  plastic sheeting
masking tape
ultramarine and sky-blue
  iron-fix silk paints
large artist's paintbrush
iron
tacking thread and sewing
  needle
one skein each of DMC
  stranded cotton in
  magenta 3804, pink 604,
  red 666, orange 721, and
  golden-yellow 972; two
  skeins of dark cream 644
needlepoint needle size 24
gold or silver coin decorations
matching sewing thread
two 10¼-inch squares of
  pink silk fabric
ready-made gold or silver
  tassels with cords

The women of the Mien people from the hills of northern Thailand set great store by their embroidery skills. Garments and accessories made from black- or indigo-dyed cotton are exquisitely embroidered with cross stitch and darning patterns. The first lesson of embroidery for a young Mien girl aged five or six is to stitch five motifs, and she will gradually extend her knowledge of pattern, drawn from a great repertoire of traditional Mien designs, as she gains in experience. The Mien people's embroideries are closely linked to their creation myths, which describe the landscape in needlework terms, for example, using pleating and stitching to represent the hillsides.

There is no set number or combination of colors used by the Mien for their embroidery, although red hues (magenta, red, pink, orange, deep golden-yellow) plus pale blue are the dominant thread colors.

❶ Place one Aida square on a flat surface covered with newspaper and plastic sheeting, and secure the edge with masking tape. Working from side-to-side, paint stripes of ultramarine paint close together across the fabric. Repeat with sky-blue paint, filling in the gaps between the stripes of ultramarine paint.

❷ Allow the paint to dry thoroughly and repeat with the second piece of Aida fabric. Press on the wrong side with a hot iron, then dip the fabric into cold water to remove any surplus dye. Pull the grain of the fabric straight and allow to dry flat. Press on the wrong side with a hot iron.

❸ Fold one Aida piece into four to find the center. Mark with two rows of tacking stitches. Work the design in cross stitch (page 17) from the center, using the chart (page 106) and three strands of thread in the needlepoint needle. Each square on the chart represents one cross stitch.

❹ Press lightly on the wrong side, then sew coins in the corner spaces. Cut the surplus fabric away around the embroidery, leaving a margin of 13 unworked fabric blocks. Cut the other Aida piece to the same size. Turn 6 blocks underneath around the edge and tack in place.

❺ Line each piece of fabric with pink silk, slipstitching the two fabrics together around the edge, and catching in a tassel at one corner of each piece. Oversew the front and back pieces together with matching thread, leaving a gap of 4¾ inches at either side of the tasseled corner.

76

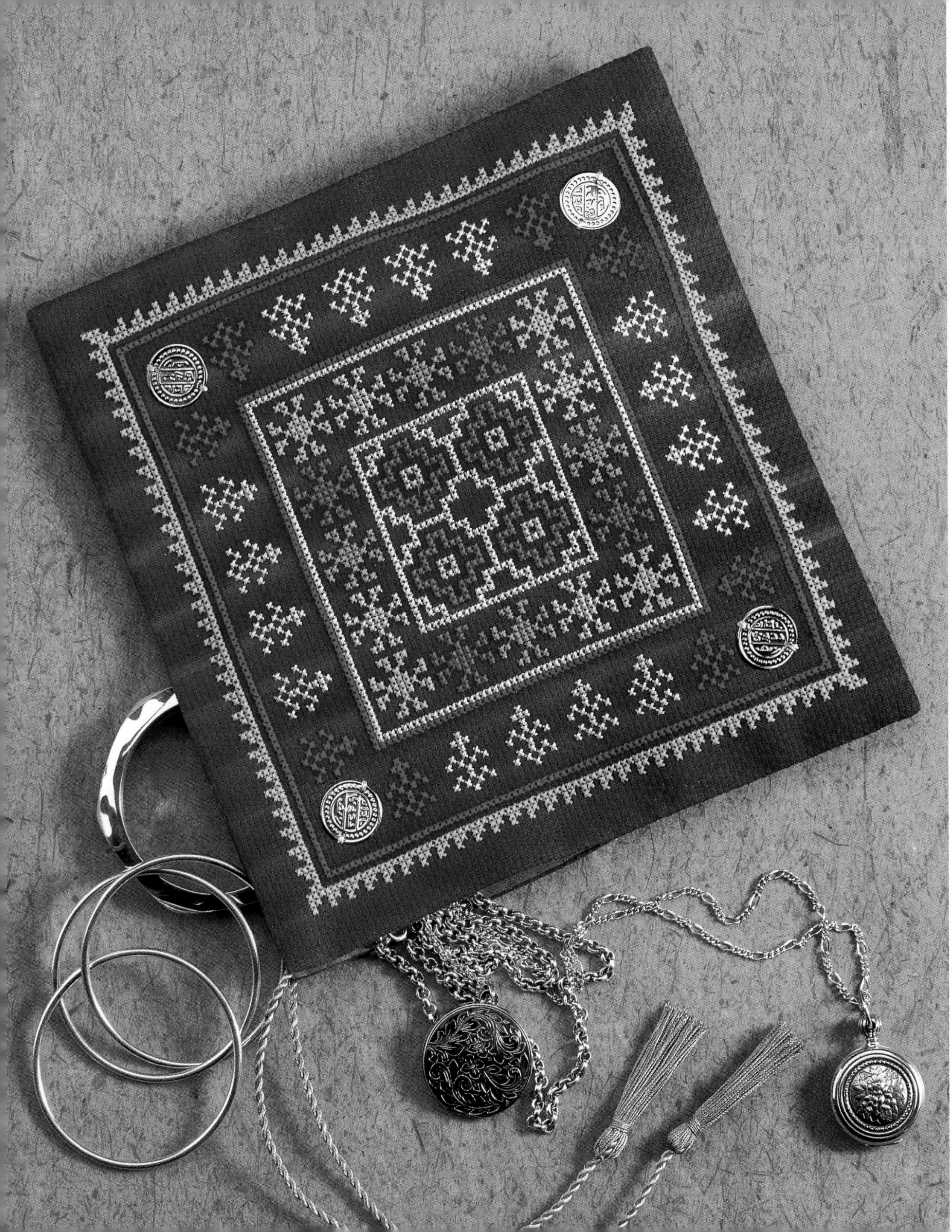

Mexican Star Weaving

You will need

two ⅝-inch thick bamboo
 skewers for each star
craft knife
cutting-mat
selection of tapestry wool in
 bright colors
ornaments as described
 opposite, four for each star
matching sewing thread and
 needle

These colorful star-shaped weavings are found throughout Latin America and, less commonly, in parts of Africa and the East. The weavings are made from yarn wrapped around a cross shape made from two pieces of smooth stick. They are known in Latin America as Ojos de Dios, God's Eyes, and are made both to symbolize an eye and to act as a request for help, care, and protection from the gods. In Mexico, a God's Eye is made for each of the first five years of a child's life; after this age, the child is thought to be able to weave its own symbol and ask for protection directly. The stars are often woven in several colors of yarn, and can be left unadorned or have objects attached to the end of each arm. Tassels, pompons, feathers, tiny bows, ribbon, beads, buttons, and small seashells are all common additions.

There are two ways of wrapping the yarn round the sticks — one method gives a flat surface which hides the shape of the cross, while in the other the cross shape shows. You can use almost any type of stick, from thin garden canes, wooden dowel, and dried twigs from the garden through bamboo skewers and cocktail sticks, but remember that the weight of the yarn should relate to the thickness of the sticks.

❷ Turn the sticks over and tie a knot at the center back, using the end of the original tail of yarn and the yarn you hold in your hand. Pull the knot tight, and do not cut the yarn. Turn the sticks over so that the knot is on the back of the cross. The side facing you is the right side and should remain facing you throughout the weaving process.

❶ Select two skewers and trim off the points with the craft knife. Make sure that both the sticks are the same length. Cross the sticks and hold them in the center with your left hand. Lay a long tail of yarn across the intersection and, holding the yarn in your right hand, lash the sticks together with a figure of eight, pulling the yarn taut.

❸ To wrap the sticks and conceal them, hold the cross in your left hand and yarn in your right. Take the yarn over and under one arm of the cross and tighten. This completes one wrapping. Continue wrapping the remaining three arms in the same way to complete one round. Repeat until the weaving is the required width, then change to the next color.

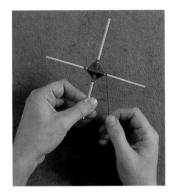

4 To wrap the sticks using the second method, proceed as before, but this time wrap the yarn under and over each stick. To join in a new color with either method, stop at the wrong side of one arm and cut the yarn to leave a 2-inch tail. Loop the tail once round the arm and tuck the tail under the loop. Pull the end tightly, knot the new yarn onto the tail, and continue wrapping as before.

5 After you have finished wrapping the star, secure the end of the yarn by cutting a 2-inch tail, and knot around the stick as before. Stitch an ornament onto the end of each arm using a double length of matching sewing thread. If you wish to hang the stars, tie a short piece of yarn around the top stick to make a loop.

Indonesian Batik Cushion Cover

You will need

15-inch square of white cotton fabric

thick transparent plastic sheeting

newspaper

masking tape

pre-cut wooden star 2 inches across (or card to cut your own template – see page 102)

cork

superglue

water-soluble marker

batik wax

small heatproof bowl and old saucepan

paintbrush with natural bristles

protective gloves

Deka 'L' or similar fabric dye in 80 cornflower blue, 83 marine blue

coarse (kosher) salt

large stainless steel or heatproof glass bowl

clean scrap paper

iron

detergent

two 8 x 15-inch pieces of dark blue backing fabric

matching sewing thread

cushion pad

Batik is a decorative process in which molten wax is applied to cotton or silk fabric to make a pattern. When the fabric is dyed, the wax resists the dye and prevents it from penetrating the fabric, allowing the background color to remain undyed. The name "batik" is Indonesian, but this process is also used extensively in India, Sri Lanka, and Thailand, Africa, and South America.

Batik produced on the Indonesian island of Java is amongst the finest and most highly decorated of all examples of the craft. Javanese batik features both natural motifs and mythological patterns, including peonies, dragons, and the tree of life. Javanese women used to wear tulis batik (hand-drawn batik patterned with a canting – a special type of bamboo pen with a copper spout) for everyday wear, but this is now a luxury kept for special occasions.

The star-and-spot pattern on this batik cushion cover is made by applying molten wax with a paintbrush to white fabric. The fabric is waxed and dyed twice, to give a white, pale blue, and dark blue pattern.

❶ Wash, dry, and press the white fabric. Lay the plastic sheeting over layers of newspaper and place the fabric on top. Secure with tape around the edges. Stick a cork onto the back of the wooden star to make a handle. Hold the star on the fabric and draw around the edge with the water-soluble marker. Repeat at random across the fabric.

❷ Pour some wax granules into the heatproof bowl and stand it in an old saucepan containing about 3 inches of simmering water until the wax melts. Leaving the bowl in the pan, dip the paintbrush into the wax, and paint the stars. Working quickly, use five strokes for each star, brushing from the tip of each arm to the center. Leave to cool.

❸ Wearing protective gloves, mix the cornflower blue dye with hot water and salt in a large bowl, following the manufacturer's instructions. Allow to cool. Remove the fabric from the plastic sheeting, dampen with cold water, and immerse in the dye for the recommended period of time. Remove the cloth, rinse in cold water, and hang up to drip-dry.

❹ Secure the fabric over the plastic sheeting and reheat the wax. Touch up any missing wax on the stars, using the paintbrush dipped in the wax. Load the brush with wax and press the tip onto the fabric to make large spots between the stars. Allow to cool, then repeat on the other side of the fabric.

❺ Leave to cool. Remove the fabric from the plastic sheeting and crumple between both hands to make cracks and creases in the wax. Shake off any loose flakes of wax. Repeat the dyeing process previously described using marine blue dye. Rinse and hang up the wet fabric to drip-dry.

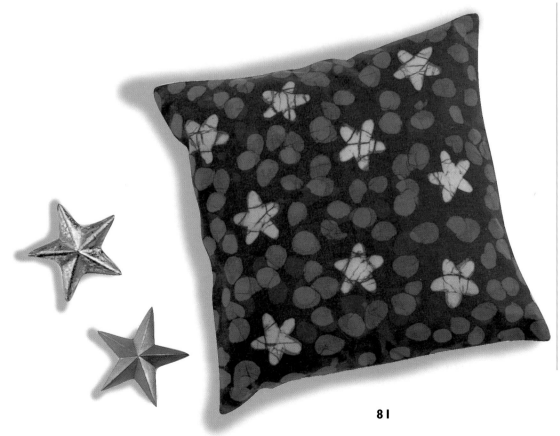

❻ Place layers of newspaper on a flat surface and cover with scrap paper. Place the fabric on top and cover with paper. Press with a hot iron until the paper is soaked with wax. Change the paper and repeat until all visible wax has gone. Wash in hot water and detergent to remove any wax. Make up into a cushion cover following Steps 3 and 4 on page 84, but leave a long opening and insert a cushion pad instead of the stuffing.

Magical Animals and Mythical Beasts

The physical strength and instincts of animals are revered by many cultures, and many animals are regarded as guides to take us to a better world. Depict a creature in your craftwork that you sense an affinity with, or whose qualities you admire.

Thunderbird

Native Americans attribute thunder and lightning to the spirit Thunderbird. Anything struck by lightning is believed to possess great spiritual power. The Thunderbird symbolizes unlimited happiness, and its tracks represent bright prospects.

Hare

The hare symbolizes love and fertility, and is linked to the goddess of dawn and spring. Hares were said to lay the decorated eggs exchanged at Easter. In China, the hare is linked with the moon.

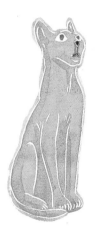

Cats

Cats represent the female, the moon, and domesticity, but also cruelty. In the West, cats were associated with Satan and witchcraft. To the ancient Egyptians, a cat symbolized watchfulness and the moon goddess, Bastet.

Elephant

Elephants stand for strength and wisdom, and are much revered in the East. Buddha is believed to have entered his mother's womb in the form of a white elephant. Ganesha, the elephant-headed Hindu god of wisdom, represents learning (see page 54). In China, elephants symbolize the energy of the universe.

Serpents

The serpent is often associated with the phallus, hidden lust, and fertility. Two serpents entwined stand for the light and dark sides of the mind. A seven-headed serpent is a symbol of the seven deadly sins, which is based on a Canaanite myth; it is also connected with the mystical number seven and represents the creative force.

Unicorn

The mythical unicorn symbolizes the moon and femininity. Its twisted horn was thought to render poisons harmless. The creature avoided all humans except virgins, and was believed to have led Archangel Gabriel to the Virgin Mary. The unicorn is often depicted with its opposite, the lion, which represents the sun and masculinity.

The Basilisk

This yellow-eyed mythical monster of the desert is a frightening creature of classical legend. At times represented more in the way of a serpent, the Basilisk had a powerful stare that would cause madness or death. Its breath alone could be lethal. The Basilisk's gaze could only be returned if the onlooker watched its reflection in a mirror.

Hanuman

Hanuman, the Hindu monkey god, denotes cunning and strength, and demonstrates the power to discipline emotions. Hanuman was a devoted servant of Rama and his wife Sita of The Ramayana.

83

Caucasian Rug Pincushion

You will need

8-inch square of 10-mesh
    interlock canvas
masking tape
8-inch square Siesta
    interlocking embroidery
    frame
push-pins
fade-away embroidery
    marker
Paterna Persian Yarn in the
    following colors: one skein
    of cobalt blue 541 and
    cobalt blue 543; two skeins
    of navy blue 571, sunrise
    812, and salmon 841
needlepoint needle size 22
two 4 x 8-inch pieces of dark
    blue corduroy, velvet, or
    heavy cotton for the
    backing
pins
matching sewing thread
white polyester toy stuffing
knitting needle
sewing needle

The exquisite patterns and harmonious colors of Persian, Anatolian, and Caucasian rugs have enchanted art collectors for centuries. Created by nomadic and semi-nomadic peoples, whose lives were often a constant struggle for survival against the elements in inhospitable country, a single rug would take many months to complete.

Rugs woven in the villages of the Caucasus mountains, running between the Black and Caspian Seas, are particularly colorful, with strong, geometric motifs and bold colors. Traditionally, every village and nomadic tribe had its own particular motifs and patterns, but with intermarriage and social contact the distinctions gradually became blurred to form a strong regional style. Flowers, animals, fruits, human forms, and everyday objects have become stylized into almost unrecognizable geometric designs, which have a life and strength that embody the people's determination to survive. The design of this needlepoint pinchusion combines stylized flower and pomegranate motifs, the latter being the symbol of happiness and fulfillment.

❶ Bind the edge of the canvas with masking tape and mount it in the embroidery frame, using push-pins. Mark the center with the marker.

❷ Beginning at the center, work the design in tent stitch (page 17) from the chart (page 106), using two strands of yarn in the needlepoint needle. Each square on the chart represents one tent stitch worked across one canvas thread.

❹ Trim the seams, clip the corners, and turn the pincushion right side outward through the opening. Stuff it firmly with polyester stuffing, using the knitting needle to pack the stuffing into each corner. Stitch up the opening to complete.

❸ Place the backing pieces together with right sides facing and long edges aligning. Make a seam along one long edge, leaving an opening of about 4³/₄ inches at the center. Making sure that the seam is in the center, place the backing and the finished embroidery right sides together and pin round the edge. Machine-stitch close to the last row of embroidery, using matching thread.

CHAPTER SIX
PaPer ChAsE

Chinese Festive Lanterns
The Magical Rainbow
Medieval Papercut Prayer
Japanese Fish Kite   *Magic Mask of Zaire*
Greek Mythology Greeting Cards
Javanese Shadow Puppet   *Symbols of Love*

Paper is a wonderfully versatile material. It can bend with the wind, curl up with a character of its own, and rustle mysteriously when moved. Since paper is often made from trees, it is no wonder that the material itself seems to hold a spirit of its own, for trees are often thought to be the guardians of spirits, sacred or even magical in their powers. Paper can also be made from other magical plants, such as the papyrus favored by the Ancient Egyptians, rice, or filled with flowers for interesting effects. Our paper projects bring creative ideas from all around the globe, with a magical papier mâché mask that can change the wearer's soul, a kite that dances in the heavens, a shadow puppet that seems to talk, and simple, deeply symbolic greeting cards.

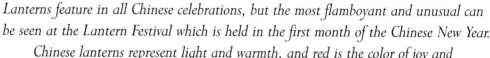
Chinese Festive Lanterns

Lanterns feature in all Chinese celebrations, but the most flamboyant and unusual can be seen at the Lantern Festival which is held in the first month of the Chinese New Year.

Chinese lanterns represent light and warmth, and red is the color of joy and celebration in China. This festive lantern is made of red tissue paper. The honeycomb effect is surprisingly easy to achieve, and the lantern folds flat when not in use.

❶ Use the template on page 104 to cut 80 lanterns from red tissue paper. To cut through more than one layer of tissue accurately, staple approximately 15 layers together.

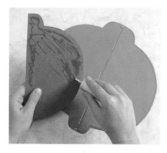

❷ Sew the layers of tissue paper together along the center. Cut two lanterns from red card, cutting along the broken lines. Glue the card sections onto the tissue with all-purpose household glue.

❸ Lift up the tissue paper halves on one side, all except the bottom one. Dab paper glue on the bottom tissue half at the dots.

❹ Press down the next tissue half and dab glue at the crosses. Continue in the same way, alternating the gluing positions, until you reach the top layer.

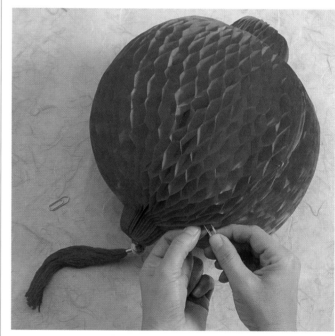

❺ Glue the other half of the lantern in the same way, then glue the top layers together at the gluing positions. Suspend a red tassel on a long length of yarn and thread on a bead. Glue the tassel yarn along the center of the lantern with all-purpose household glue.

❻ Bring the card halves together and secure with paperclips to hold the lantern open. Suspend the lantern on red yarn.

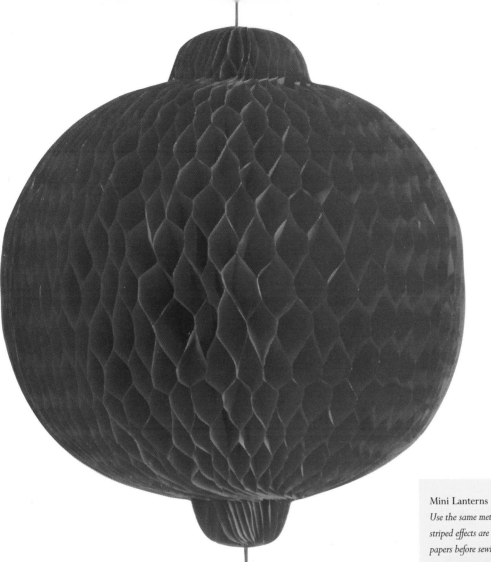

Mini Lanterns
Use the same method to make miniature lanterns. Colorful striped effects are created by layering different colored tissue papers before sewing the lanterns together.

89

The Magical Rainbow

The rainbow, that most spectacular spectrum, has inspired legend down the centuries —
unsurprisingly, since its exact nature, involving almost all there is to know about light, has
remained inexplicable until recent times. What better source of color symbolism can there
be for creative use in craftwork. Choose appropriate hues from the magical rainbow to bring
extra meaning and spiritual significance to your crafts.

Violet
Violet is the most important color of the
rainbow, lying at one end of the visible
spectrum next to blue. It is a vital color
for meditation. Violet flowers represent
true love and mourning.

Orange
The word for the color derives from the
fruit, probably orginating from the Sanskrit
word meaning "fruit approved by
elephants." In the Orient, orange
represents love and happiness. Its sense of
warmth has obvious associations with
sunsets, flowers, and orange-skinned fruits.

Yellow
Yellow was the national color of China. In Buddhism, it is symbolic of humility and
renunciation. In many cultures, yellow represents the rising sun in all its power, and for
the Native Americans, it also stands for wisdom, equality, and the eagle.

Rainbow Symbolism

The rainbow is an important symbol of communication because it links the earth to the heavens. Some African cultures see the rainbow as a conduit of energy between the two. Norse gods constructed a rainbow bridge between the earth and their home, Asgard. The rainbow represents the forgiveness of God in Christianity because a rainbow appeared after the Great Flood.

Indigo

Indigo is regarded as a highly sacred color. Many customs must be adhered to when producing indigo as a dye. In Nigeria and Indonesia, a chicken feather is suspended over the dye pot to protect it from evil.

Blue

The color blue has strong meanings in Christianity. It is the color of the Virgin Mary, compassion, faith, and baptismal waters. Blue conjures up thoughts of peace and contemplation, and it represents the sky, water, and infinity.

Green

Green has obvious connections with spring and nature. To the Native Americans, it stands for Mother Earth, the sustainer of life. Green also denotes youthfulness.

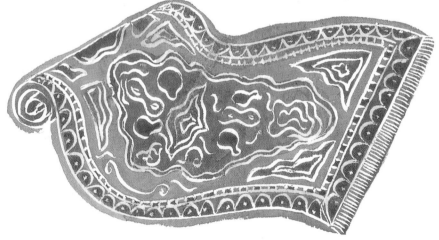

Red

In ancient Persian and Turkish carpets, red was the predominant color used to create their beautiful, intricate designs. In this context, red represented joy and happiness. To Native Americans, red stands for strength and loyalty, and symbolizes the bear.

Medieval Papercut Prayer

You will need

tracing paper
black craft paper
ruler
pencil
masking tape
cutting-mat
craft knife
dressmaking pin
spray-glue
cream-colored card

Intricate papercuts are created all over the world. Chinese papercuts are thought to bring good fortune and prosperity. They are cut with delicate knives and colored with inks before being hung at windows or given as funerary gifts.

In South America, the Aztecs made paper from bark known as amate, from which they cut stylized figures. These were then used in religious rituals. A Mexican tradition still practiced today is called Papel Picado – colorful tissue papercuts are displayed at weddings and Day of the Dead festivals. Wycinanki is the Polish craft of papercutting. Colored papers were originally cut with sheep shears to make Easter decorations.

This stylish papercut is based on the German art of Scherenschnitte, which evolved from the cutwork prayer pictures of medieval monasteries. Scherenschnittes were later given as love tokens, the heart being a popular motif.

❶ Enlarge and trace the template on page 102 onto tracing paper. Cut a rectangle of black paper 6³/₄ x 5¹/₄ inches. Use a ruler and pencil to draw a line on the rectangle, dividing it lengthwise in half. Fold in half along the division.

❷ Tape the tracing face downward onto the folded paper, matching the straight line to the fold. Redraw along the outlines to transfer the design. Remove the tracing.

❸ Working on a cutting-mat, carefully cut out the design with a craft knife. Make sure the blade is sharp so that the cut is neat and smooth. Start at the corners when cutting the inner shapes.

4 Pierce the dots with a pin, then gently open the design out flat. Run your finger along the fold to flatten it. Spray the back of the papercut with spray-glue, and attach to a piece of cream-colored card, smoothing the papercut outward from the center.

Love Token

When cut from watercolor paper, the scherenschnitte can be delicately painted. The tub has been omitted from this version of the design, which would make a lovely greeting card.

Japanese Fish Kite

pencil
A3-size layout paper
scissors
craft paints
paintbrushes
medium-gauge wire
paper glue
yarn or thick thread

Kite-flying in Asia is not regarded as a child's pastime. Kites are flown at many festivals, most having religious connections. Fantastic bird- and animal-shaped kites are believed to possess evil spirits that float away from the kite owner's family. Other kites are used for fighting tournaments.

In Japan, a carp-shaped kite is flown at the Boy's Festival on May 5 for every male child. It is hoped that the boys will take on the worthy characteristics of the fish — overcoming difficulties while swimming upstream. This kite is not intended for flight but would make an impressive decoration to hang on a wall or door. Brightly painted, the open mouth is wired to hold its shape.

❶ Draw a carp 16 inches long on layout paper. Add a strip ⁵/₈ inch wide to the mouth end as a channel for the wire. End the channel ³/₈ inch inside the top and bottom edges of the fish.

❷ Cut out a pair of carp kites, and fold under the channels.

❸ Paint the carp, adding details with a fine paintbrush. Leave to dry.

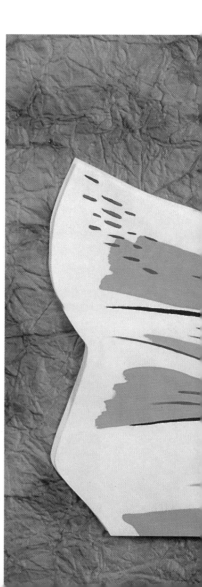

94

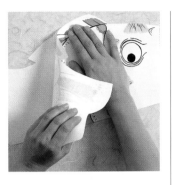

❹ Slip a length of wire under the channel of one kite section, leaving 1 inch extending at the start. Glue the channel to the kite, enclosing the length of wire.

❺ Place the folded edges of the kite sections together. Lay the wire inside the remaining channel and glue. Cut off the excess wire leaving 1 inch extending. Twist the ends.

❻ Glue the outer edges of the two kite sections together with the wrong sides facing, leaving the wired mouth of the kite open.

❼ Gently squeeze the mouth to round it. Tie the ends of a length of yarn to each side of the mouth.

Magic Mask of Zaire

You will need

thin card
pencil
ruler
plastic clay
rolling pin
small, pointed knife
petroleum jelly
newspaper
PVA medium
flat paintbrush
kitchen paper towels
scissors
cream-colored latex paint
fine sandpaper
soft cloth
raw sienna acrylic paint
polyurethane matte varnish
jute or string
all-purpose household glue

Masks have a place in most societies. In Greek theater and the Noh plays of Japan, masks symbolize the qualities of the characters that they represent. In Sri Lankan theater, masks represent demons.

Because they hide personal identity, masks are often believed to take the wearer to a higher state or to allow spirits and gods to work through them. The ceremonial masks worn in New Guinea by young men to mark the end of childhood have long grass skirts attached to completely hide the wearer.

African masks were worn to protect against enemies and to summon ancestors. Those made of wood were greatly prized, and marked the wearer's status within the community. This mask is inspired by the wood and fiber masks of eastern Zaire. It can be made inexpensively from papier mâché.

❷ Roll a large piece of plastic clay out flat to ³/₈ inch thick, and lay it across the top of the mask as a forehead. Trim away the excess clay around the outside, and cut away an arched eyebrow on each side of the center line.

❸ Cut out two long, almond-shaped eyes from the remaining clay and set aside. Cut the edges of the forehead diagonally to slant them. Smooth along the edges of the forehead with a finger to curve them.

❺ Place the eyes on the mask, cut the edges diagonally with a knife, then smooth the edges in the same way as the forehead. Rub petroleum jelly on the mask mold – this will act as a releasing agent.

❻ Tear newspaper into strips ³/₈-1 inch wide. Mix PVA medium with a little water until it has the consistency of light cream. Brush the solution onto the strips and lay them smoothly on the mask, overlapping the edges of the paper and extending them beyond the edges of the mold.

❶ To make a mold for the mask, cut an oval from thin card 13¹/₂ inches long by 8¹/₂ inches wide. Cut the lower edge slightly narrower for the chin. Draw a line lengthwise along the center. Pull the ends between a thumb and finger to curve them upward. Rest the ends of the mask on plastic clay to maintain the curved shape.

❹ Roll a long cylinder of clay for the nose, then roll the top to taper it. Squeeze the cylinder to a triangular shape and lay it along the center line, with the tapered end against the forehead. Smooth onto the forehead and the card with a finger, and mold the lower end to a point.

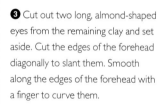

❼ With the mold still resting on the plastic clay, continue building up layers of papier mâché, laying each layer in a different direction to the last for strength. Using a different colored paper for each layer of paper mâché helps to differentiate one layer from another.

8 Leave to dry after you have applied 12 layers of papier mâché. Draw around the outer edge of the mold on the underside. Pull away the mold and wipe off the petroleum jelly. Cut out the mask. Cut out the eyes and a mouth.

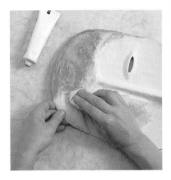

9 Paint the mask with three coats of cream-colored latex paint, sanding the surface lightly before the final coat. Use a soft cloth to rub on raw sienna acrylic paint. Apply varnish.

10 Glue long lengths of jute or string to hang from the lower edge. Braid three lengths of jute together, knotting the ends to start and finish. Glue over the jute ends on the mask, and cut off the knots.

97

Greek Mythology Greeting Cards

Myths are symbolic stories to be interpreted by the society in which they occur. All civilizations have their own myths, and ancient rulers often embellished these myths to include themselves, so that they would be regarded as more than mere mortals.

Greek mythology has provided inspiration for arts and crafts for centuries. These classical stenciled greeting cards feature the god of love, Eros, and a bountiful cornucopia. Eros is portrayed with his traditional bow and arrow, since this arrow will be sure to reach the hardest of hearts! He is sometimes shown blindfolded to show that love is blind. This card would be great to give to a valentine or as a wedding anniversary card.

The cornucopia, or horn of plenty, belonged to Amalthea, a nymph in the form of a goat who suckled the god Zeus. A goat's horn was thought to give fertility. The horn represents the union of man and woman, and will bestow endless riches.

You will need

blue card
craft knife
steel ruler
cutting-mat
stencil board
masking tape
flat paintbrush
gold craft paint
ceramic tile or old china plate
stencil brush

❷ Use the templates on page 103 to draw the stenciling designs onto stencil board. Cut out the cut-outs using a craft knife and working on the cutting-mat.

❶ Cut a rectangle of blue card 12 × 8¼ inches for each card. Using a craft knife and steel ruler, and resting on a cutting-mat, score crosswise across the center of the card. Fold the card in half along the center.

❸ Tape the designs to the front of the cards. Apply a thin film of gold paint to a ceramic tile or an old plate with a flat paintbrush. Holding the stencil brush upright, dab at the paint.

❹ Dab the paint through the cut-outs, still holding the brush upright and moving it in a circular motion to distribute the paint. Leave to dry, then peel off the stencil.

Symbols of Love

All cultures have fascinating folklore regarding affairs of the heart. Lovers have exchanged keepsakes and tokens of love for centuries. Making a gift for a loved one is a wonderful way of showing that you care, and will be much treasured by the recipient.

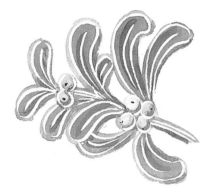

Mistletoe

Mistletoe represents the female. It was worshipped by pagans, who believed it had links with fertility. It also featured in Druid ceremonies. A popular custom today is for a girl and boy to kiss under sprigs of mistletoe.

Heart

The heart is the most common representation of love. It also stands for compassion and sincerity, and is the source of all emotions. A winged heart is a symbol of Christ, and a flaming heart denotes Venus, the goddess of love.

Spoons

Spoons are exchanged as love tokens in many cultures. Beautiful carved wooden spoons are given in Wales, Russia, and Zululand – the wood represents the Tree of Life. Silver spoons represent purity and chastity.

Sun and Moon

The sun symbolizes the male and, as a sustainer of life, was worshipped as a god in many cultures. The sun denotes desires of the heart in astrology.

The moon is said to be female and, because of its cyclical nature, stands for immortality and resurrection. The waxing moon represents regeneration and female fertility. Farmers often sow seeds under a waxing moon to encourage germination. The new crescent moon has links with the Virgin Mary and ancient Egyptology.

Love Knots

Like the wedding ring, a love knot is a sign of eternity. The endless knot denotes eternal love and longevity. Japanese love letters are written on paper that is folded and then knotted. A blue knotted ribbon represents lovers.

99

Javanese Shadow Puppet

You will need

pencil
thick, ivory-colored card
water-based felt-tip pens
plastic carrier bag
liquid paraffin
kitchen paper towels
craft knife
cutting-mat
thick needle
thick thread
wood dowel ¹/₄ inch in
    diameter
hand-drill

Puppets are thought to have originated in the East. China had shadow puppet theaters in the 10th century. Java also has an ancient shadow puppet tradition, in which the puppets are animated behind a white sheet with a light behind them. The plays are based on Hindu mythology. The story of Rama rescuing his beloved Sita is a popular tale of good and evil.

Javanese puppets are often grotesque. This is thought to be because the Javanese were converted to Islam and so were forbidden to make human images. Shadow puppets are traditionally made from animal hide. The skin is scraped and stretched, then dried to create a parchment-like material. Sharp chisels are used to make patterns of holes on the painted puppets to let the light shine through them. This puppet is made from card treated with liquid paraffin to make it translucent.

❶ Use the templates on page 104 to draw the puppet onto the card. Color the with water-based felt-tip pens, allowing each color to dry before using a different color against it. Add details with fine-tipped pens. Leave to dry.

❷ Cut open a plastic carrier bag to protect your work surface, and lay the card on top. Rub liquid paraffin into the puppet with a kitchen paper towel until translucent.

❸ Turn the card over and rub paraffin into the other side. The color will begin to show on this side too. Wipe away excess paraffin with a clean kitchen paper towel. Apply paraffin to any areas you have missed.

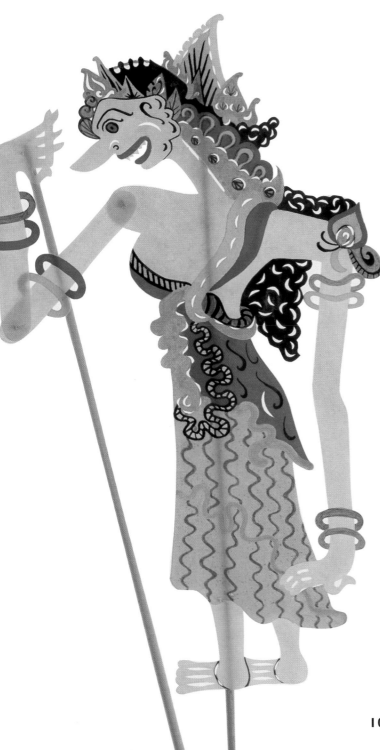

4 Using a craft knife and resting on a cutting-mat, cut out the puppet sections. Cut away small areas outlining the design for the light to shine through them.

5 Make a hole at the dots. Thread a needle with a double length of thick thread. Insert the needle through the shoulder and top of the upper armhole. Knot the threads securely over the holes, and cut off the excess thread. Join the forearm to the upper arm in the same way.

6 Cut a piece of dowel 20 inches long and another 17 inches long. Drill a hole 1/4 inch from one end of each piece of wood dowel.

7 Thread the needle with thread and insert through the hole on the headdress, bringing the needle out on the back of the puppet. Thread the needle through the hole in the long stick. Knot securely over the hole. Attach the short stick to the hand in the same way.

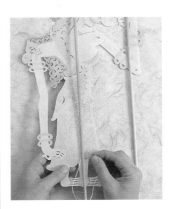

8 Lay the long stick along the body, and oversew it to the puppet with a few stitches.

Templates and Charts

The following pages present the templates for many of the projects. Apart from the Hand of Fatima Amulet, the templates will need to be enlarged. Using the percentage specified, enlarge each template in size on a photocopier. To make a complete pattern for the Chinese lantern, cut out the template and place on a piece of folded paper matching the "place to fold" line to the folded edge. Cut out and open out flat to use.

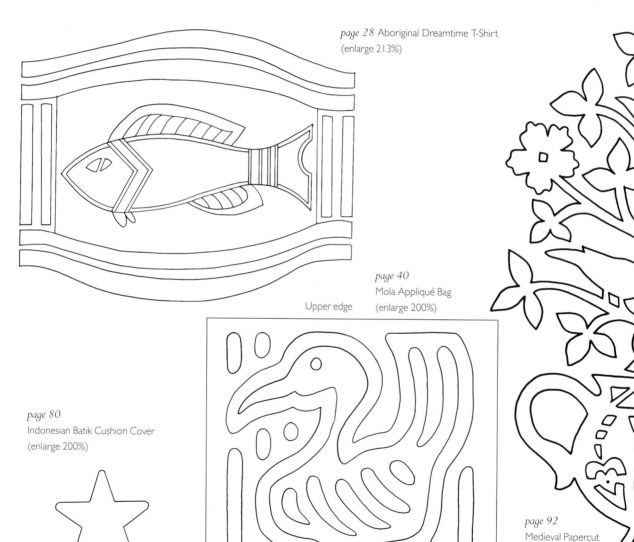

page 28 Aboriginal Dreamtime T-Shirt
(enlarge 213%)

page 40
Mola Appliqué Bag
(enlarge 200%)

Upper edge

page 80
Indonesian Batik Cushion Cover
(enlarge 200%)

page 92
Medieval Papercut
Prayer
(enlarge 165%)

page 36
Morning Star Pendant
(enlarge 110%)

page 38
Hand of Fatima Amulet

page 98
Greek Mythology Greeting Cards
(enlarge 168%)

Place to fold

Upper arm

Forearm

page 88
Chinese Festive Lanterns
(enlarge 217%)

page 100
Javanese Shadow Puppet
(enlarge 204%)

page 70
Rooster Weather Vane
(enlarge 223%)

Eye

page 50
Navaho Sand Painting Scarf
(enlarge 192%)

page 84 Caucasian Rug Pincushion

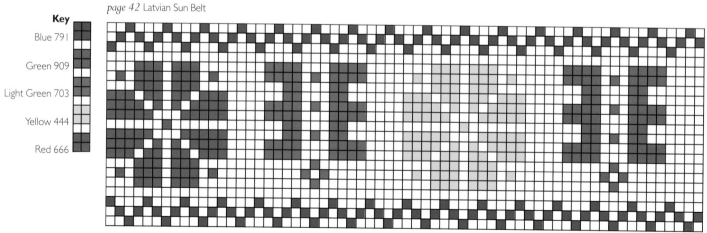

¹/₄ repeat

Key

Paterna: 812 Sunrise

Paterna: 571 Navy Blue

Paterna: 541 Cobalt Blue

Paterna: 543 Cobalt Blue

Paterna: 841 Salmon

page 76 Mien Jewelry Bag

¹/₄ repeat

Key

Dark Cream 644

Magenta 3804

Pink 604

Red 666

Orange 721

Golden Yellow 972

page 42 Latvian Sun Belt

Key

Blue 791

Green 909

Light Green 703

Yellow 444

Red 666

Index

Author's Acknowledgments

The author would like to extend special thanks to Jan Eaton for creating the beautiful projects on pages 28-29, 36-37, 42-43, 50-51, and 76-85.

Grateful thanks also to: DMC for supplying stranded cotton, Aida fabric, and interlock canvas.
Paterna for supplying Paterna Persian Yarn.
Candle Makers Supplies for supplying candle-making, fabric painting, silk painting, and batik materials. Their materials are available by mail order from 28 Blythe Road, London W14 OHA, UK, tel: 011-44-171 602 2796.